People Who Have Helped the World

RALPH NADER

by Kelli Peduzzi

For a free color catalog describing Gareth Stevens' list of high-quality children's books, call 1-800-341-3569 (USA) or 1-800-461-9120 (Canada).

Picture Credits

The Bettmann Archive — 11 (upper right), 27, 32, 34; Cindy Lewis Photography — 5; map by Sharon Burris, © Gareth Stevens, Inc., 1989 — 8; © Karalee Helminak, 1989 — 52; Lake County (Illinois) Museum, Curt Teich Archives — 7, 10, 13, 24, 35, 48; Photo courtesy of Milwaukee County Historical Society — 29; © Harry Quinn, 1990 — cover; Torrington Register Citizen — 54, 55; UPI/Bettmann Newsphotos — 4, 6, 14, 16, 17, 18, 19, 21, 23, 25, 31, 33, 37 (both), 43, 51, 59; U.S. Department of Agriculture — 11 (lower left), 19, 22, 47; Wide World Photos — 40.

A Gareth Stevens Children's Books edition

Edited, designed, and produced by
Gareth Stevens Children's Books
RiverCenter Building, Suite 201
1555 North RiverCenter Drive
Milwaukee, Wisconsin 53212, USA

Text, end matter, and format copyright © 1990 by Gareth Stevens, Inc.

First published in the United States and Canada in 1990 by Gareth Stevens, Inc.

Library of Congress Cataloging-in-Publication Data

Peduzzi, Kelli.
    Ralph Nader / by Kelli Peduzzi.
        p. cm. — (People who have helped the world)
    Includes index.
    Summary: A biography of the consumer advocate who devotes his life to crusading for citizens' rights, such as safer cars, cleaner food, and truthful advertising.
    ISBN 0-8368-0098-2
    1. Nader, Ralph—Juvenile literature. 2. Consumer affairs directors—United States—Biography—Juvenile literature. 3. Lobbyists—United States—Biography—Juvenile literature. 4. Consumer protection—United States—Juvenile literature. [1. Nader, Ralph. 2. Consumer affairs directors. 3. Consumer protection.] I. Title. II. Series.
HF5415.5.N33P43 1989 343.73'07'0924—dc19   [B]   [92]   89-4282

Series conceived by Helen Exley
Series editor: Rhoda Irene Sherwood
Research editor: Kathleen Weisfeld Barrilleaux
Picture researcher: Daniel Helminak
Layout: Kristi Ludwig

Printed in the United States of America

1 2 3 4 5 6 7 8 9 96 95 94 93 92 91 90

RALPH NADER

Crusader for safe consumer products and lawyer for the public interest

by Kelli Peduzzi

Gareth Stevens Children's Books
MILWAUKEE

Unsafe at any speed

"For over half a century the automobile has brought death, injury, and the most inescapable sorrow and deprivation to millions of people." So began a book called *Unsafe at Any Speed*, published in November 1965. This book exposed for the first time the truth behind many highway traffic fatalities.

By February 1966, the first printing of nine thousand had been sold; by August 1966, twenty thousand of the second printing were sold, and the book was on the best-seller list. The author of this book had made a revolutionary claim. He accused automobile manufacturers of making poorly designed cars that increased a passenger's chances for injury in an accident. He blamed them for placing more importance on looks than on durability. He accused Ford, Chrysler, American Motors, and General Motors (GM) of failing to use technology that was already available to improve safety. He claimed they were sacrificing human lives to make huge profits.

The frightening Corvair

His careful research into the car industry revealed disturbing facts about the way cars were made. He asserted that one particular car, the Corvair, was so badly designed that it was causing more deaths on the highway than any other car. The Corvair had a tendency to roll over, he said. The manufacturer had deliberately sacrificed safety for sporty looks so it could sell more cars.

Since the model's appearance on the market in 1959, 106 owners of Corvair cars had filed lawsuits against General Motors totaling forty million dollars in damage claims. The car was unstable, they said. It would spin or roll over at the slightest bump in the road. In cases where head-on collisions occurred, the

Opposite: Ralph Nader first testified before a U.S. Senate committee about unsafe cars in 1966. Angry about the design and production of some cars, he insisted that consumers had a right to know about a car's safety performance.

The Corvair, subject of Ralph Nader's investigation.

Nader watches as an "air bag" device prevents injuries to a little girl during a safety test. Nader urged Congress to pass a law requiring air bags in all new cars, but pressure from automakers blocked the bill.

"That's the sixth one this month. I tell you, Dan, there's something wrong with the Corvair. I don't know if it's that rear engine or the crazy suspension, but that's six cars that should never have been in accidents."

A California highway patrolman to his partner, quoted in Richard Curtis's Ralph Nader's Crusade

---

Corvair's steering column lunged into the driver's chest, pinning and even killing the driver.

Highway patrol officers noticed the large number of injuries and fatalities in the Corvair in even minor accidents. Never before had anyone blamed a car's design for *causing* injuries and death.

Now here was an unknown lawyer, doing just that, a young lawyer named Ralph Nader.

Milking the public

In the late 1950s, Nader had become curious when he learned the number of deaths in the United States occurring in automobiles. Surely all the accidents couldn't be due to bad driving, he thought. There must be something wrong with automobile design. And so began his research.

In *Unsafe at Any Speed*, Nader concluded that automakers were intentionally designing cars with a higher risk of accident and with no safety features. He recommended seat belts, impact-absorbing bumpers, and padded dashboards to protect people from fatal head injuries.

Moreover, he argued, so many car accidents were creating an entire service economy — the medical, police, legal, insurance, repair, and funeral professions — and these people were milking others of billions of dollars. It was preposterous! Cars were obviously designed to cost consumers as much money as possible, not to safeguard their lives.

A conscientious lawyer, he backed up his arguments with facts. There was no question about it. General Motors, the producer of the Corvair and the largest American automaker at that time, was selling a dangerous car. It was not providing for consumer safety and was responsible for injury and death, yet nobody was holding GM accountable.

That GM could get away with this outraged Nader. It made him angry that GM made billions of dollars selling its cars, yet invested very little to do research into auto safety.

The shocking truth

One of the facts he uncovered was that after making 1.7 *billion* dollars in profit in 1964, GM had allotted only one million dollars for safety research, a mere fraction of a percent of its revenue. And safety research was clearly needed.

So GM was not just negligent. It was also greedy. The angry young lawyer hammered home the fact that car owners paid GM a considerable amount of money to own one of its death machines and then had to pay again for medical, funeral, and other expenses when accidents happened, accidents that drivers could avoid if cars had decent suspension systems and crash-proof front ends.

Nader summoned all his moral indignation to proclaim that "the true mark of a humane society must be what it does about *prevention* of accident injuries, not the cleaning up of them afterward." He hoped his book would publicly expose GM and inspire the public to demand safety features in its cars.

Of the copies of his book that sold, one found its way into the offices of the General Motors Corporation in Detroit, Michigan. What the automobile executives read made them very uncomfortable.

What does Ralph Nader know about automotive design? they thought. Is he a witness in one of the lawsuits against us? He wants to make us look bad in front of the public and to discredit our product. What if the public actually listened to him? Our sales could really be hurt, and we could lose a lot of money.

Just who is this Ralph Nader? they wondered. Where did he get the authority to accuse us of endangering public safety?

"When he sees that 50,000 people die in auto accidents, he doesn't see a number. He sees 50,000 individual people."
Laura Nader, Ralph Nader's sister, quoted in Richard Curtis's Ralph Nader's Crusade

"You pay ten cents for a cup of coffee and you also get a dollar's worth of talk."
Former customer of the Highland Arms, quoted in Hays Gorey's Nader and the Power of Everyman

Driver safety warnings like this one from 1960 were correct in warning drivers to be responsible when driving. But the people who issued them seemed ignorant of the hazards posed by the cars themselves, such as a lack of seat belts.

BE AWARE
BE ALERT
THINK ONLY OF DRIVING !
In Case of EMERGENCY — Read REVERSE Side
BE COURTEOUS
BE SAFE

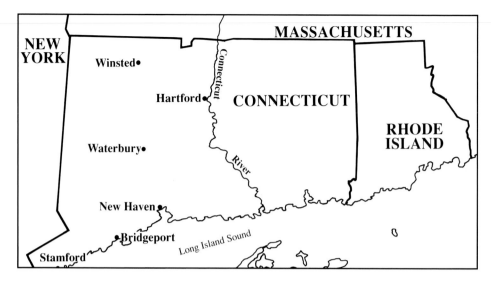

Winsted, Connecticut, is a small town in the north-western part of the state.

Nathra Nader

Ralph Nader was born February 27, 1934, the youngest of four children. His parents, Nathra and Rose Nader, emigrated from Lebanon to America in 1912, in search of political and economic freedom. They also wanted their children to have decent educations and economic opportunities. After a few years in New York, the Naders settled in a comfortable house in Winsted, Connecticut, a town of 10,000 working-class people.

Nathra, Ralph's father, was no stranger to work. Across the street from their home, he opened a restaurant called The Highland Arms. There, he dispensed generous helpings of food along with his numerous — and strongly held — opinions about the ways of the world. Customers at The Highland Arms always knew they would get an earful of talk as well as a plateful of food!

Nathra was famous in Winsted for appearing at town meetings. He would demand information about how the taxpayers' money was being spent and would have his say on what the town ought to do to solve problems. Ralph went with his father to these meetings, fascinated by what his father was saying.

All of Ralph's childhood and youth, his father was full of advice. He told his children not to believe in heroes, because it was better to rely on yourself than

> *"My father used to tell me what lawyers* **could** *do compared to what they* **did** *do. He took a very public-spirited view of things, and I learned that the legal profession was the most flexible, most catalytic spot from which to try to improve society."*
> Ralph Nader, quoted in Richard Curtis's Ralph Nader's Crusade

to rely on a hero. "It is the individual's duty to speak out," he would say. "A good system is here [in America] . . . but it will not work by itself. We have to make it work." Or he might assert to the children, "A citizen must give more to his country than he takes from it." And about freedom, he would say, "What is the value of freedom if people don't use it?"

Nathra prized freedom of speech and passed this respect for freedom to each of his children — along with passionate caring for others. Ralph listened to his father, taking every lesson to heart.

Rose Nader

Rose Nader stayed at home while her children were growing up because she felt they needed constant support and encouragement. There were four of them: Shafik, the eldest, had been born in Lebanon. Then came Claire, Laura, and finally Ralph.

Rose was strict. Everything her children did had to have educational value — even when they went to the movies. If the children asked to go to a movie, she would question everyone who had seen it. Only when she was satisfied that the children would learn something would she let them go. If her children ever complained about something, she would tell them to stop complaining and *do* something about it.

But Rose was also kind. She impressed upon her children how important it was to *care* about other people. Throughout their childhood, she was a great source of strength for her children.

She also raised them to be independent. Like Nathra, she never talked down to the children but, instead, treated them as adults and expected very grown-up behavior.

For instance, Nathra and Rose insisted that the family have dinner together every night. At the dinner table, Nathra would begin the meal by asking a question. "What if," he would say, and he would pose a problem for the family to solve. He expected everyone to participate in the discussion and also expected them to be able to defend their opinions. When the six very opinionated and talkative Naders gathered for dinner-table discussions, the talk often lasted long after dessert and into the night.

"We couldn't just complain. If we said we didn't like something, we were told to do something about it."
Laura Nader, quoted in Hays Gorey's Nader and the Power of Everyman

"I taught Ralph to be human, to think of others before he thought of himself. This, I think, is the essence of his appeal."
Rose Nader, quoted in Robert Buckhorn's Nader, the People's Lawyer

"Even if you were hurt, you were not allowed to run under fire; it was not appropriate to quit. You had to argue for the position you had, but the wonderful thing was that nothing said, no matter how heated, was allowed to disturb the family relationship. But if you couldn't stand the truth, you didn't ask Dad."
Claire Nader, quoted in Robert Buckhorn's Nader, the People's Lawyer

The ivy-covered walls of Blair Tower loom like a medieval castle over Princeton University's campus, where Ralph attended college from 1951-55.

Ralph and his brother and sisters all say that the dinner-table episodes had a strong influence on them when they grew up. For Ralph, especially, it was where he learned to argue for his point of view, using facts to back up the argument, a skill that he would use every single day of his adult life.

The serious boy

Nader became fascinated with the law at a young age when he could often be found at the town courthouse listening to lawyers argue cases in front of the jury. His parents didn't mind that he lingered at the courthouse. In fact, they encouraged this curiosity, for like his brother and sisters, he was a bright child.

Ralph watched and listened. He remembered his father's telling him that if he wanted to make any kind of lasting changes in the world, becoming a lawyer was the best way to do it.

Ralph never even questioned the necessity of making the world a better place in which to live; it was something he'd been brought up to do. So from an early age, he decided he would be a lawyer.

When most of his friends were outside playing ball, Ralph could be found inside reading the *Congressional Record*, an enormous book that even lawyers read only when they have to. All of his teachers remember him as a very quiet, serious, studious boy.

First taste of the world

Upon graduating from high school in 1951, Ralph attended the graduation ceremony only to please his parents, since he regarded it as a waste of productive time. The next fall, he entered Princeton University. His parents had carefully saved money for his education, as they had for his brother and sisters, because education was important to all the Naders.

Once at Princeton, however, Ralph decided most of the other students were frivolous. He thought they were concerned only about who they were seen with, what they wore, and what they drove. Ralph preferred to stay up all night reading everything he could get his hands on. And he remembered most of what he read.

In time, Ralph gained the reputation around school for being shy and reclusive. He made few friends because, as he once said, "most people didn't stay up all night."

The friends he did make, though, knew that Ralph wasn't shy at all. True, he didn't talk about things like himself, dating, or sports (although he did memorize the ball scores every day). But if he started discussing a subject he cared about — such as politics or his major in Oriental studies — watch out! He would never shut up.

In 1962, Rachel Carson wrote Silent Spring, *the book that exposed the dangers of pesticide spraying. The government banned use of the chemical DDT because of her discovery that it deformed and killed birds and caused cancer in humans as well.*

The beginnings of the advocate

On the parklike Princeton campus, Ralph noticed that the trees had been sprayed with the pesticide DDT, and many birds lay dead from DDT poisoning. If birds were dying from DDT, Ralph reasoned, people could die too.

So he wrote a letter to the Princeton newspaper about the situation and demanded that the use of dangerous chemicals cease on the campus. The paper refused to print the letter. He was astonished at the indifference of those around him to the obvious hazards in their environment.

Years later, in 1962, Rachel Carson would publish an influential book titled *Silent Spring.* Carson proved the dangers of DDT and warned

Ralph Nader says that pollution is a consumer issue because people cannot avoid drinking, eating, and breathing industrial pollution and toxic wastes. He insists that industry take the responsibility for paying its share of the cost to clean up the environment it has been poisoning.

11

against human tampering with the environment. Shortly thereafter, the government banned DDT. Meanwhile, Ralph wondered why it was that others saw only some dead birds when he saw the effects of deadly poison.

The disappointed idealist

When Ralph left Princeton in 1955, he again graduated with high scholastic honors. And again, he attended the ceremony unwillingly, just to please his proud parents. Perhaps these early doubts were part of his skepticism about institutions.

Years later, for instance, he was unexcited when Princeton called him the graduate "who had done the most in the nation's service." He wrote to Princeton's college newspaper that Princeton had not contributed to his life's achievement. "You develop in spite of — not because of — any institution," he maintained, always saying exactly what was on his mind.

In the fall of 1955, Nader eagerly entered Harvard Law School, bent on becoming a public-interest lawyer. Harvard was known throughout the world as a fine school. But again what Ralph found there surprised and disappointed him. Almost all of the law courses were about business and corporate law. His classmates seemed determined to study law so they could manipulate it for rich clients who could pay them high fees.

"It was the worst conceivable distortion of legal education," said Ralph. "They were training us to be experts in servicing big businesses. In the meantime, the problems of the cities were building up, racial problems were building up, environmental problems were building up, bureaucracies were building up. And we weren't even exposed to these as challenges to our profession."

These were the problems, Ralph Nader had grown up believing, that the law was designed to correct. It was not meant to serve the interests of the wealthy and powerful. He became bitterly disillusioned with Harvard, doing only the minimum of work to get his law degree. He became more determined than ever to use the law to serve the public interest in ways that were being ignored at Harvard.

Hitchhiking to a cause

What Ralph couldn't learn from courses at Harvard, he would teach himself. He devoted himself to reading the law on his own, particularly in the area of social issues. When he wasn't reading or working to make a little money, he was hitchhiking around the country, trying to see as much of it as he could.

It was during these hitchhiking episodes that his interest in highway safety began. As he rode along, he would see terrible accidents happen and would see people who were badly hurt.

He took it upon himself to interview every truck driver he rode with, asking about the safety of their vehicles. To his astonishment he discovered that drivers had often been injured because of the poor design and construction of their vehicles. Why, in one truck he had ridden in, a sharp bolt was sticking out right where the driver might hit his head against it — and often did, so he was told.

Making a name for himself

Ralph turned his experiences on the road into an article for the *Harvard Law School Record* published on December 11, 1958. It was called "American Cars: Designed for Death." It was followed a few months later by "The Safe Car You Can't Buy" which appeared in a magazine, *The Nation*. He received requests from all over the country for copies of the articles. Nader had found a hearing with the public. He was becoming an advocate.

He graduated from law school absolutely refusing to attend what he regarded as a meaningless ceremony. The diploma was just a piece of paper, he said. His education would really mean something only if he used it to change the system that badly needed setting straight.

After Harvard, Nader spent six months on active duty in the Army Reserve as a cook. His discharge papers stated that his equivalent civilian occupation would be that of "executive chef." The army didn't notice that its chef hung around the jeep garage to stay up on automotive trends. Despite the role the military had assigned to him, Ralph Nader was moving out in the world ready to start making it work!

The truckers Nader met when crossing the country undoubtedly saw many warnings such as this. Not until Nader's work roused them to anger, however, did the public decide that being a well-instructed driver wasn't enough. They wanted well-constructed vehicles.

"Without rights, democracy cannot exist, but without rights linked to remedies represented by lawyers, a practically functioning democracy cannot exist, and that is what the great gap is in this country."
Ralph Nader, quoted in Robert Buckhorn's Nader, the People's Lawyer

From Connecticut to Washington

After law school, Ralph returned to Connecticut, this time to one of its largest cities, Hartford. Determined not to serve the interests of big business, he worked in the humble law offices of George Athanson.

While he was there, people kept coming to him with small grievances against government agencies. They were just getting pushed around by the bureaucracy, they complained. Could he help?

Their situation was intolerable to a man like Ralph Nader, who felt compelled to act on even the smallest problems. He decided to create an American ombudsman system, a system whereby people represent individuals who have complaints.

The bill he drafted to this effect and set before the Connecticut legislature in 1963 was not well received and did not pass into law. But it represented an early attempt by the young Nader to address the problems of ordinary citizens.

In the meantime, Nader had been corresponding with Daniel Patrick Moynihan, then assistant secretary of labor under President John F. Kennedy. Ralph had first noticed Moynihan's writings on tire safety while he was still at Harvard, and they wrote regularly back and forth on the subject.

Nader found practicing law in Hartford frustrating. He wasn't involved in any big issues that would bring about changes in the system. When Moynihan offered Ralph a job as consultant to his agency, Nader moved to Washington, hoping to pursue his interest in auto safety full-time.

But despite his cordial working relationship with Moynihan, Ralph still wasn't satisfied with his own progress in forcing change on the auto industry. "I decided what it took was total combat," he later said, and left the consulting job to devote all his time to researching the problem of dangerous car design.

It was at this time that he began intense work on the problem of the Corvair, and it was this work that in 1965 produced *Unsafe at Any Speed*, the book that made GM executives nervous. After the publication of this book, sales of the Corvair plummeted 93%. What, the executives asked themselves, were they going to do about this man Ralph Nader?

Daniel Patrick Moynihan, assistant secretary of labor in 1965, was Ralph Nader's first important friend in Washington, D.C. He invited Nader to come and work for him on auto safety investigations.

GM's secret investigation

The GM executives eventually came up with a solution that they thought would solve their problem. They hired private detectives to follow Ralph Nader and report back on everything he did.

The detectives were instructed to find out something about Nader that GM executives could use against him, something scandalous or dishonest that they could wield as a weapon to publicly discredit him. They hoped that they could damage Nader's reputation. Then they could point to *Unsafe at Any Speed* and say, "Look at the kind of man who wrote this. You can't believe someone like him. He can't prove any of the statements in this book."

Ralph Nader began to notice odd happenings as he went about his daily routine, both at home and at the Senate office building in Washington, D.C., where he was preparing to testify at upcoming hearings on highway safety.

Young women he had never met would approach him in the supermarket and invite him back to their apartments. Anonymous callers would repeatedly phone him as he tried to work. He once received six such calls in one day!

His friends and employers told him that they were also receiving anonymous phone calls asking about his private life and especially about his driving record. He had the creepy feeling he was being watched. But why?

General Motors executives spent thousands of dollars and many months trying to find something incriminating about Ralph Nader, but the only thing they could tell about him was that he lived a very simple, quiet life in a run-down rooming house.

He didn't drink alcohol, didn't gamble, and didn't smoke. There was no evidence that he even went out on dates. He seemed to have very little money. He certainly wasn't working for any of GM's competitors or for any of the people bringing lawsuits against the company. In fact, Ralph Nader, whoever he was, seemed to be working solely for the sake of public health and safety.

This puzzled the GM executives and, in time, they ordered the detectives to halt their investigation.

"He seems to be a bit of a nut or some kind of a screwball."
Richard Danner, attorney for General Motors, quoted in Robert Buckhorn's Nader, the People's Lawyer

"The key to living an exciting professional life is to live a dull personal life. Why is it supposed to be so much more pleasurable to watch a movie or a football game or listen to music than to protect the consumer interest?"
Ralph Nader, quoted in Hays Gorey's Nader and the Power of Everyman

"He's an original. There's no one like him anywhere in the world. And I mean that in the finest sense. No single individual has done more to dramatize the interests and needs of the ordinary citizen."
Senator Abraham Ribicoff, quoted in Hays Gorey's Nader and the Power of Everyman

Senator Abraham Ribicoff led the congressional investigation on highway safety in 1966 during which Nader first gained fame. He alerted Nader when he learned that Nader was being tailed by detectives in the nation's Capitol.

"Ralph Nader is perhaps the single most effective antagonist of American business."

Associate Justice
Lewis F. Powell, Jr.,
U.S. Supreme Court, quoted
in Hays Gorey's Nader and
the Power of Everyman

Brought to justice

But it was too late. Senate security guards had seen the detectives trailing Nader into the U.S. Capitol building as he entered to testify on auto safety. The guards quickly ejected the suspicious men and told Senator Abraham Ribicoff what they had witnessed.

Ribicoff was leading the Senate's investigation into highway safety in which Nader was testifying. It is a federal crime to harass, impede, or intimidate a congressional witness, and Ribicoff knew it. He suspected the men of doing just that and told Nader, confirming Ralph's suspicion he was being spied on.

Then a *New York Times* story in March 1966 accused GM of spying on Nader. The public had never heard of this Nader fellow, but they sure knew the car maker. The rumor of a giant corporation's investigating a private citizen drew unpleasant attention to GM, which flatly denied what it had done.

GM's denial angered Nader. With Ribicoff's help, he brought his case against GM to the Senate Subcommittee on Executive Reorganization in the spring of 1966. This subcommittee was conducting the hearings on highway safety. Led by Ribicoff, it evaluated the government's role in improving highway and traffic safety. Nader had spent months working with the subcommittee on research.

One of the first witnesses at these hearings was the chairman of General Motors, James Roche. While Roche was testifying about auto safety, Nader presented him with evidence that GM had conducted the secret investigation of his private life. An embarrassed Roche, one of the most powerful people in America, had no choice but to apologize publicly to an ordinary, private citizen.

GM apologizes publicly

"Let me make clear at the outset that I deplore the kind of harassment to which Mr. Nader has apparently been subjected," Roche said. "I am just as shocked and outraged by some of the incidents which Mr. Nader has reported as the members of this subcommittee [are]. I did not know of the investigation when it was initiated and I did not approve it. I am not here to excuse, condone, or justify in any way our investigating Mr. Nader. To the extent that General Motors bears responsibility, I want to apologize here and now to the members of the subcommittee and Mr. Nader. I sincerely hope these apologies will be accepted. Certainly I bear Mr. Nader no ill will."

The public was shocked! The chairman of America's most powerful corporation had not known what his staff was up to? They were more shocked that the investigation rumors turned out to be true.

James Roche, then chairman of General Motors, insisting that he had no knowledge of GM's spying activities, apologized publicly to Ralph Nader.

An awakening

As the newspapers ran stories about the incident, the public suddenly realized that this man named Ralph Nader had been working to protect their very own interests. He was fighting to protect their lives and rights as consumers. Maybe with Nader leading the fight, they would get fewer cars that maimed and killed people.

When *Newsweek* ran a cover story about him in March of 1966, Nader became an instant symbol of the ordinary citizen's power. His name became a household word. He stood for the public interest, uncompromising integrity, and the power of the individual to improve society.

The American public immediately claimed Nader as their representative because he worked on the problems that most frustrated them. They saw how he made real progress because he was brave enough, bold enough, and smart enough to stand up to the powerful corporations. Ralph exposed their secrets, their lying and cheating. He blew the whistle on them when they broke the law.

Seeing the public rally to his side, Ralph Nader wasted no time in suing General Motors for the invasion of his privacy. Nader asked for $26 million in damages, but the corporation settled the suit out of court, giving Nader $425,000. Corporate executives hoped the money would convince him to go away quietly so that the public would forget the whole matter and go back to buying cars.

Never had anyone underestimated a person the way GM had Ralph Nader. Nader was not about to

"True, he does what he does out of a compulsion. But he just loves it. He is having a ball."
Reuben Robertson, attorney at the Center for the Study of Responsive Law, quoted in Robert Buckhorn's Nader, the People's Lawyer

"GM can be caught lying and making defective cars, but if Nader is caught just once on something big, he will be destroyed."
A Washington lobbyist, quoted in Robert Buckhorn's Nader, the People's Lawyer

give up the fight once he saw the giant General Motors Corporation forced to admit it was wrong, especially when Americans took Ralph's side. In one stroke, this quiet, serious lawyer had brought America's largest corporation to its knees and the public was not about to forget it. Those hearings on highway safety, by the way, resulted in the passage of the Traffic and Motor Vehicle Safety Act of 1966.

How a public citizen spent $425,000

When GM executives paid $425,000 to Ralph Nader, they thought the world had heard the end of the upstart young lawyer, but in fact the money launched a long public career. Since his days at Harvard, Ralph had dreamed of starting a public-interest law firm where lawyers would work only on consumer issues. He envisioned an organization that would be a center for the development of policies to protect public interests, not business interests.

The money in his pocket provided the perfect opportunity to act on this dream. He would hire talented experts in engineering, medicine, chemistry, and biology to lead investigations in their respective fields. Ralph himself would be the unpaid chairman of the board.

Ralph Nader appears in a familiar pose behind a forest of microphones at a meeting of Public Citizen, one of nineteen consumer groups that he started.

Fees that Ralph made for giving speeches, profits from the sale of his book, and money from grants and foundations helped fund his investigations.

When the public heard what he was doing, contributions came in from everywhere. Rumpled dollar bills came through the mail — even a $100,000 check from a wealthy businessman! To Nader, the public was using its financial support to say, "Work for us. Help us. We need you."

The "career of citizenship"

The firm would operate on Ralph Nader's most strongly held principles. Most important, the firm would stage an organized, systematic crusade for the power of the individual to make a difference. It would encourage people to exercise their freedom of speech, and by doing so, they would reclaim their role in government. A true, working democracy, Ralph believed, was possible only when the governed participated in the process that governed them.

He would work to instill in the public mind the importance of being a vigilant consumer. He would also try to show how important it was for workers to "blow the whistle" on employers who knowingly endangered lives or the public safety.

"As more individuals become disillusioned with decisions that have ravaged our economic and physical environment," says Ralph, "they find they can no longer remain silent. If an employee brings a safety or health hazard to the attention of superiors and it is ignored because profit is placed above public safety, it becomes the employee's duty to go outside the corporate structure and reveal the hazard. . . . There is no excuse for 'following orders' if those orders harm others."

The center's lawyers would share Ralph Nader's disgust for the way powerful institutions cheated the public. They would work to spread the idea that citizenship was not just a right — it was a duty.

They would work to prove that government and corporations had citizenship duties too. They had to be held accountable for their actions. Citizens deserved to know the facts about concerns directly affecting their lives.

"Working for Ralph gives you a feeling of power. You walk into someone's office, and you can almost see [that person] sweat. It isn't a nice feeling, though. It's rather frightening. Many corporations are running scared, and the officer you talk to knows that not only his job but also the stock of the company, and maybe the company itself, is on the line."

A Nader's Raider, quoted in Richard Curtis's Ralph Nader's Crusade

A seemingly beautiful park in Little Rock, Arkansas, contains a dire health warning. Nader urges us to eliminate the causes of such pollution or we will more and more frequently suffer consequences like this.

The Center

In May of 1969, Ralph Nader established the nonprofit, tax-exempt Center for the Study of Responsive Law (CSRL), or The Center, as it is known. He hired six eager young lawyers to start investigating a number of weighty problems.

Headquarters was a decaying nineteenth-century, red brick mansion in Washington, D.C. No signs marked the building to tell passersby what was inside. The lawn was unkempt. Inside, piles of old newspapers and cardboard boxes full of files vied for space with worn furniture. Under glaring fluorescent light, two telephone switchboards constantly buzzed.

Upstairs in the offices, padlocks were put on the doors to protect the valuable — and usually incriminating — information within. There was almost no heat in winter. Ralph's office had piles of books taking up floor space and a picture of Thomas Jefferson pinned to the wall.

In 1971, the building was demolished to make way for the new subway system, but the new Center headquarters on Nineteenth Street proved to be about the same. It was modern and had heat, but existed in the same state of controlled clutter as the original.

Meet Nader's Raiders

Despite Ralph's disdain for Princeton and for Harvard's law school, most of the firm's early members had attended one or both of these schools and were Ralph's good friends. Among them were William Taft IV, great-grandson of President William Howard Taft, and Edward Cox, son-in-law of President Richard M. Nixon.

His Princeton and Harvard friends may have gone to elite schools and may have thought they could profit from the reputation of those schools, but Nader made no bones about what he expected of his young "Raiders," as the press called them. He would pay them about half of what they could expect to earn in a corporate law firm, and the hours would be long — sometimes sixteen hours a day.

They would probably have to work on weekends if they expected to get their projects done by the deadlines, and never mind about taking a vacation.

"We play by the rules every step of the way. And there is very good reason for doing that. You can get what you want that way. If you don't play by the rules, your credibility is going to be destroyed by personal attack."
Harrison Wellford, CSRL associate, quoted in Robert Buckhorn's Nader, the People's Lawyer

"If they're willing to work for what I pay them, then they're genuinely interested. If they're not, then there are other places they can go."
Ralph Nader, about offering Raiders low pay, quoted in Richard Curtis's Ralph Nader's Crusade

20

They would be expected to develop their own projects independently and to be able to conduct investigations on their own. They would not be allowed to lean on him for guidance.

"I'm looking for self-starters," Ralph lectured. "I don't want people who have to be constantly told to do this, or do that. Anybody can work for me who has the ability to dig up facts, the ability to interview, can meet deadlines, and, most of all, is self-reliant."

Ralph Nader talks to students at the Illinois Public Action Council in Champaign, Illinois, in 1984. Nader wants more Americans to become what he calls public citizens, *people who become actively involved in local issues in order to bring about change.*

No glamour job

The Raiders would have to absorb volumes of detailed information by reading every important document. Every fact was ammunition in the fight.

They would have to conduct hundreds of interviews to get information from the target itself. They would have to be fearless in pursuing people who would rather avoid them. Finally, they would have to turn their findings into reports that would publicly expose whatever industrial or bureaucratic crime the investigation was aimed at.

The job sounded demanding, but also thrilling. But it was not as thrilling as it seemed. In fact, many Raiders resented their nickname, saying it gave the public a false sense of glamour about them.

"We are not raiders. That is a very inaccurate name. When you are sitting there at two o'clock in the

"The image [of this being glamorous work] is so far off! . . . It's working long hard hours, reading day after day what is boring — trivia, hearings, memos, letters, scholarly treatises. It's just hard, tedious work."
A Nader's Raider, quoted in Richard Curtis's Ralph Nader's Crusade

In 1970, sights like this reminded Nader that public action is meant to reach not just corporations and government bodies but also the private citizen who litters the environment in this way. Recycling trash cuts down on ugly litter like this and makes the cost of manufacturing aluminum cans lower.

morning, going over documents page by page . . . thousands and thousands of pages, compiling things, gathering evidence, talking to people, you don't feel like a raider at all. You feel like a scholar," said Robert Fellmeth, an early member of the Center.

A tenacious staff

In the years since 1969, Nader's well-educated, diligent staff has investigated grievances about countless shoddy products and suspect practices. Where there were no safety standards, Nader and his Raiders investigated products to expose their poor quality and dangerous construction. Where products harmed consumers, they demanded that corporations be held responsible for damages. They wanted to be sure that industry obeyed the laws that governed them, so when industries broke the law, the lawyers publicly exposed them.

As far as Nader was concerned, all industries were fair targets for his scrutiny. But so were government agencies that did not do a decent job of monitoring health and safety standards. Nader's aim in

investigating was to protect the public from waste, fraud, exploitation, and danger.

Sometimes Nader worked eighteen hours a day, seven days a week, to expose the injustices played on a trusting public. The Center branched out into other areas besides auto safety. It investigated pollution, food, chemicals, clothing, work-place safety, and even government ethics. Nader's outrage — so easy to arouse when he uncovered deception and greed — was infectious.

The consumer revolution

In the 1960s, Nader and his Raiders launched the consumer revolution. Corporate America watched as citizens all over the country began a wave of consumer unrest. These citizens demanded that their cars be made better, that their food be made more wholesome, that their prescription drugs be put in safety bottles, that their toys and clothes be made safer, that their air be made more clean.

They listened as Nader told them that they, too, could make a difference. They didn't have to be the

"I've got to set a very high standard. If I ever have to ask someone to work on New Year's Eve, I want them to be sure that I have already done 17 times more work on the project than I am asking them to do."
Ralph Nader, quoted in
Robert Buckhorn's
Nader, the People's Lawyer

"Individuals still count. They can generate a momentum for change; they can challenge large and complex institutions; there still is a very critical role for citizen action and for the development of citizenship that will improve the quality of life in the country."
Ralph Nader, quoted in
Robert Buckhorn's
Nader, the People's Lawyer

Senator Warren G. Magnuson displays scorched children's pajamas at the Senate subcommittee hearings on the Flammable Fabrics Amendments of 1967. Because of such hearings, the law now requires all children's pajamas to be flame retardant.

23

This gruesome scene from a mine explosion in 1912 recalls the days before tightened safety standards. Such sights are now less frequent.

victims of shoddy automobile design or poisonous air pollution. All citizens had to do was raise their voices and demand better solutions. This was the true spirit of democracy, when the governed themselves decided the laws and standards that governed them.

While people disagree on how much impact Nader's work had on every one of these issues, many believe that the investigations and the public response to them hastened the passage of laws that safeguarded citizens' lives.

Some of these laws, passed as the Center was being established, were the Freedom of Information Act of 1966, the Wholesome Meat Act of 1967, the Natural Gas Pipeline Safety Act of 1968, the Radiation Control for Health and Safety Act of 1968, the Wholesome Poultry Products Act of 1968, the Coal Mine Health and Safety Act of 1969, and the Occupational Health and Safety Act of 1970.

Nader and his group ferreted out the secrets that corporations so desperately wanted to keep hidden. The things he discovered shocked Americans, as he knew they would. His discoveries also pleased them because Ralph's determination to expose the truth made industries face up to their dishonest ways.

People began to feel they were no longer at the mercy of big business.

Of course, Nader's reports made him very unpopular with some of the leaders of these industries. They thought he was trying to tell them how to run their businesses. But Ralph didn't let their disapproval stop him. He continued to work at changing the laws that would protect the public interest. And the public continued to support him.

Students in the revolution

As part of their work, lawyers at the Center lead a team of student investigators. Despite the low pay, long hours, and grueling working conditions, Ralph discovered to his intense satisfaction that every job opening at the Center received at least a hundred applications from eager students.

Their enthusiasm for public-interest law was, he believed, proof that his basic principles were correct: people did believe that the individual could make a difference and they were acting on that belief in increasing numbers.

Ralph Nader's crusade was part of the general atmosphere of the time. The late sixties was a time in

"Control the outrage, but don't suppress it. Your outrage must be considered fuel that doesn't quite surface, but must be the metabolism of your energy. But don't spill it out until you're behind that typewriter, white-hot, putting out that memo or that final product."
Ralph Nader, about how to be a Raider, quoted in Robert Buckhorn's Nader, the People's Lawyer

Nader and young women from Miss Porter's School discuss their campaign to expose poor conditions in nursing homes for the elderly. "This is a case of the very young reaching out to help the very old," said Ralph.

America's history when students, blacks, women, and antiwar protesters took to the streets to protest injustices they saw in society.

The students applying to Ralph Nader believed they too could make a difference to society. They wanted to change the world for the better, and Nader seemed to offer a really effective way of doing it.

In one summer, the students learned the single most important lesson about consumer advocacy from Ralph. They learned that the system wasn't as hard to crack as they had thought.

To their surprise, they realized that by looking for their target's neglected and weak spots, they could uncover a lot more information and be a lot more effective than if they confronted it with a bunch of hotheaded demands.

The students learned not merely to accuse but to be armed with the facts, as Ralph had advised them. Ralph knew the value of facts. He could rattle off dozens of facts to prove any case. His energy inspired them, and they tried to copy him.

PIRGs

Nader saw his movement gain momentum with the influx of student interest. He used some settlement money to start a second consumer-advocacy law firm, the Public Interest Research Group, called PIRG. (In total, Ralph would start nineteen different consumer organizations over the years.)

The law firm's most important mission was to build a network of PIRGs in other states and to increase the number of public-interest lawyers that were independent of the Center.

Colleges around the country started their own PIRGs at Nader's urging. Millions of college students, he reasoned, would gladly pay $5 a year in support of public-interest research. The money was pooled to hire young public-interest lawyers and scientists at low rates who would, in essence, work for the causes that were of most concern to the students.

The success of Public Interest Research Groups was proof to Ralph Nader that grass-roots citizen activism could work and did work. He had only to set an example to get citizens started.

One begins to wonder why Americans hadn't been roused to action before. Why had this urgent need for a reform movement come about as late as the middle of the twentieth century? How had innocent consumers become helpless victims of unsafe and unwholesome industrial practices, and why hadn't industry, advertising, and government been held accountable for their actions long before?

Beginnings: the Industrial Revolution

History shows that the problem slowly emerged as America grew. America was not always the land of big business and advertising, says Doris Faber in her book, *Enough! The Revolt of the American Consumer.* Just over a century ago, most people lived in rural areas where they made their own food, clothing, and tools, or bartered with others who made them. People knew who they were buying the goods from and how they were made. The biggest factories were just small shops where articles were crafted by hand.

This began to change in the 1860s, when America's Northern states went to war against its Southern states. The Civil War increased the demand for ammunition and guns and also for soldiers'

At the height of the Industrial Revolution industry used children as cheap labor. This young girl and many thousands like her worked for pennies a day. While parents were horrified at the dangerous working conditions for their children, they were often powerless and poor immigrants who needed the income earned by their children. It was not until the middle class became alarmed by conditions for such children that laws were changed to regulate child labor.

uniforms. Until that time, clothing had no standard sizes. Everyone had clothes made by hand to fit personal measurements. But the huge demand for uniforms resulted in the creation of standard patterns and sizes. By the end of the Civil War, an industry existed for ready-made men's clothing.

By the 1880s, the notion of things being ready-made had become very popular. The Industrial Revolution was in full swing in North America and Europe. Machines were now used to produce most of the things that people had formerly made by hand. Factories could produce goods cheaply, quickly, and consistently. Since more goods could be made for less cost, a huge new market in machine-made goods grew up. The people who made things by hand the old way simply couldn't compete with the price and quality of factory goods, nor could they keep up with the increasing demand.

Machines proved to be adaptable to many uses so that factories made a large variety of goods that had never before been available. Ready-made goods were not just cheaper, people soon realized, but also far more convenient. People were attracted to products advertised as being time-saving gadgets, new and improved, or miraculous cures.

It seemed obvious to everyone that machines represented progress; they were going to make life easier and better. People began to value articles made quickly in a factory more than articles crafted slowly by hand, even if the factory-made thing looked like thousands of others.

More and more people moved away from the country to find work in the booming factories. The new city dwellers did not have time or space to grow their own food or make their own clothes. Many more factories grew up to meet a rising demand for more and cheaper consumer goods.

Rising consumer frustration

Business had become a huge and impersonal exchange. No longer were customers also the neighbors down the road. Now, customers were people the factory owners did not know. Besides, there were many more customers now than there had been before factories existed. More things were being bought. Factories made their owners very rich.

The businessmen soon saw that they could make even more money by using cheaper materials in their product and charging the same amount as they would for the better product. They also promised that new medicines and machines would do miraculous things for people. This encouraged innocent people, who bought the products because they did not know the manufacturers were lying. And business owners became even richer.

Consumers soon noticed that products began to break shortly after they were bought. Even worse, many businesses claimed their products did things that they failed to do. But what could a consumer do about these dishonest promises and badly made goods? The businesses were too big and powerful for a customer's protest to have any effect. Besides, there was no law to prevent businesses from making a product and advertising it any way they wished.

The makers of Cornea Restorers guaranteed a cure for every imaginable eye disease. Phony cures like this were common in the days before consumers spoke up against companies that cheated and harmed them with useless, unsafe products.

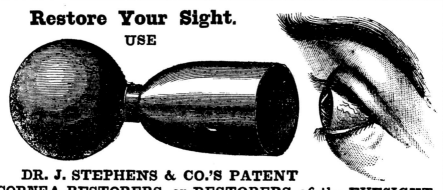

Restore Your Sight.
USE

DR. J. STEPHENS & CO.'S PATENT
CORNEA RESTORERS, or RESTORERS of the EYESIGHT.

They will Restore Impaired Sight, and Preserve it to the Latest Period of Life.
SPECTACLES RENDERED USELESS.

The most eminent Physicians, Oculists, Divines, and the most prominent men of our country, recommend the use of the CORNEA RESTORERS, for Presbyopia, or Far or Long Sightedness, or every person who wears spectacles from old age; Dimness of Vision, or Blurring; Overworked Eyes; Asthenopia, or Weak Eyes; Epiphora, or Watery Eyes: Pain in the Eyeball; Amaurosis, or Obscurity of Vision; Photophobia, or Intolerance of Light; Weakness of the Retina and Optic Nerve; Myodesopia, or Specks or Moving Bodies before the Eyes; Ophthalmia, or Inflammation of the Eye and Eyelids; Cataract Eyes; Hemiopia, or Partial Blindness; Sinking of the Eyeball; Strabismus, or Squinting, &c.

They can be used by any one with a certainty of success, and without the least fear of injury to the Eye. More than 5000 certificates of cures are exhibited at our office. Cure guaranteed in every case when applied according to the directions inclosed in each box, or the money will be refunded. Write for a Circular—sent gratis. Address DR. J. STEPHENS & CO., Oculists, at RUSHTON'S Family Drug Store, No. 10 Astor House, Broadway, New York. (P. O. Box 926). Dr. J. STEPHENS & Co. have invented and patented a MYOPIA, or CORNEA FLATTENER, for the cure of NEAR-SIGHTEDNESS, which has proved a great success. Write for a Circular.

The only recourse a buyer had against inferior goods was to boycott (refuse to purchase) the product again. Still, it was maddening to have bought something only to discover later that you had been cheated. The more money they wasted on products that didn't perform as their makers claimed they would, the more consumers became frustrated. But no laws existed to prevent dangerous or perfectly useless products from being sold.

There were no laws because the problem hadn't existed before factories had. It was a completely modern phenomenon. Consumers had no one to turn to who could make big business pay attention to their problems. They felt helpless and angry.

An early consumer advocate

Then some people began to do research and to express their concern about the quality of products offered to the public. Dr. Harvey W. Wiley, at the chemistry division of the United States Department of Agriculture, was among the first to be concerned about food additives. In 1883, as he examined foods, he noticed that chemicals were being added to foods like meat and dried fruits. These chemicals were added to keep the food looking and smelling fresh.

Concerned about the effect of these chemicals on human health, Wiley demanded that the government set standards for food purity. He recommended that the government conduct testing of food to be sure that producers complied with the rules.

But Wiley could not convince the government of the dangers of additives. Both government officials and business told him that the rules he wanted would only interfere with the right of business to conduct free enterprise. So from his position as chief chemist at the Department of Agriculture, Wiley began speaking out publicly for the removal of impurities and additives from food.

To prove his theory, he conducted a series of experiments. To see the effect on their health, he fed a group of volunteers — known as the "Poison Squad" — food that contained additives. When the results of the tests were published in 1902, the public created an uproar of protest against food

"The biggest problem in dealing with the government is the fact that 99% of the people don't want to be bothered."
Ralph Nader, quoted
in Rolling Stone

additives. The additives had seriously affected the appetite, digestion, and general health of some volunteers, Wiley claimed.

In Chicago, a man named Upton Sinclair was about to make an even more startling announcement.

The Jungle

In February 1906, Sinclair published a book describing the filthy conditions in Chicago meat-packing plants. This book, *The Jungle*, became a huge best-seller. People were horrified to discover that the meat they ate was mixed with dust, rodent hair, and even animal excrement.

In response to the panic that followed, President Theodore Roosevelt sent a team of agriculture officials to Chicago to confirm Sinclair's story. They discovered he had told the truth.

By June, Congress was swamped by public cries of outrage, inspired by *The Jungle*, about conditions in the meat-processing plants. Over much protest from the meat industry, which thought that the

Opposite: In 1967, two famous consumer advocates meet. Nader greets Upton Sinclair, author of The Jungle. *Sixty-one years after this book first exposed the unsanitary conditions in meat-packing plants, Sinclair and Nader witness the signing of the Wholesome Meat Act.*

government was interfering with their right to conduct free enterprise, Congress passed the Pure Food and Drug Act.

Consumers were finally satisfied that their food would be properly monitored for cleanliness and wholesomeness. But Dr. Harvey W. Wiley was not. Under pressure from the angry businessmen, the new law contained a critical compromise. Yes, it required honest labeling of what was in the food, but it covered only meat that was transported across state lines. How could the new law really protect people if it did not cover all foods people would buy?

Brane-Fude

Wiley wanted to test the new law. So he brought a lawsuit against a drug manufacturer named Robert N. Harper, who made a product called Brane-Fude. Harper made elaborate promises that Brane-Fude cured headaches and actually nourished the brain.

In February 1908, Harper was found guilty of violating the Pure Food and Drug Act. Wiley had shown that Harper was making false claims about his product and misleading the public. He was given only a light fine of $700 and no jail term, but Dr. Wiley's claim against him had set a precedent. For this, Wiley became known as "the father of the Pure Food law," but there were still no rules that dictated what a product *should not* contain.

Changes in America

Such complaints against products became more common until, in 1914, Congress created the Federal Trade Commission to guard against unfair business practices. The FTC also monitored the advertising industry for misleading and fraudulent practices.

After World War I ended in 1918, Americans tried to isolate themselves from the rest of the world community. They had suffered huge losses of people and resources. Now they wanted to forget the horrors of war and rebuild the nation.

America entered "the roaring twenties," a time of almost childlike abandon in the pursuit of money and pleasure. America became a nation of consumers. But in October 1929, the stock market on Wall Street

crashed. What had been millions of dollars in investments was now worthless paper.

Factories and banks failed. Millions were thrown out of work. People guarded every cent they earned and became even more concerned when a product did not perform as they were led to believe it would. In some cases, products were even deadly, yet no law required the labeling of ingredients on the package.

This alarming situation changed for the better on June 25, 1938, when Congress suddenly passed the Food, Drug, and Cosmetic Act in reaction to a national drug manufacturing scandal.

A drug company had sold a drug whose recipe contained an experimental painkiller. When it was dissolved in another chemical, the two made a deadly poison. In all, 107 died. Even doctors prescribing the drug were unaware of the poison because no detailed labeling appeared on the package.

Congress passed the law over the loud and powerful objections of the drug companies. The law would be too much interference in their business, they claimed. Congress decided there was such a thing as enterprise that was too free.

The fact that some drug makers were not concerned if their products accidentally killed people prompted Congress to make them take responsibility for how their products were made. Their products

During the Great Depression of the 1930s, many Americans were unemployed, destitute, hungry. Sights like this long line at a free soup kitchen were common.

would have to be tested for safety and effectiveness before the drug companies could sell them. Drug companies would have to respect consumers.

Postwar consuming grips America

America entered World War II in December 1941. Food, fuel, and consumer goods became scarce as industry geared up to produce military equipment and goods for the soldiers. Even clothing and shoes were now rationed.

When the war ended in August 1945, Americans began an era of huge consumer spending to make up for what they had gone without during the war. They wanted bigger and more elaborately designed cars. Women and men wanted complete new wardrobes every year, even if their old clothes were not worn out. They wanted fancy new electrical appliances that saved household labor.

Everything had to be shiny, new, and expensive looking. Americans bought and bought and bought. They traded in last year's car for the new model, even if the "old" car ran perfectly well. The need to consume replaced the need for the object itself.

The advertising industry began to study this phenomenon. It studied the psychology of people to see why they bought things. It learned that they could use this psychology in advertising.

"If you saw them putting nine teaspoons of sugar into your soda, would you drink it?"
Ralph Nader, quoted in
The Washington Post

After the hardships of the Depression and World War II, Americans went on the biggest shopping spree in history. They bought big, shiny cars and new wardrobes every year.

Advertising began to tell people that buying a product might make them younger, more popular, more attractive. Of course, no product could guarantee these farfetched promises, but advertising could sell a lot more products by making people worry about their self-image instead of the actual product. Advertising preyed on the public's deepest feelings of fear and inferiority, and people believed it.

Then, in 1957, a man named Vance Packard published *The Hidden Persuaders*, which exposed these hidden advertising techniques. The public, Packard claimed, was being manipulated into buying things it might not need and might not even want.

Notice, sometime, how even today, advertising appeals to how a product makes us *feel* more than to how it functions.

Consumer advocacy reawakens

For the first time, consumers began to be upset about advertising. People began to fear that they were just pawns in a very large corporate game to get everyone to spend a lot of money. People also noticed that products they spent so much on were not made well. Usually they worked for a while, but then broke down very soon and required expensive repairs.

Customers found it extraordinarily difficult to return an appliance for repairs, since the company that sold the appliance often never told the customer what to do in case it broke down. If a customer could find no one to fix it or if fixing it cost so much that buying a new one would cost only a little more, the old one was thrown out, a new one was bought, and the cycle started all over again.

The poor customer was left to solve the problem alone. All that corporations seemed to care about was making money.

Most people had never heard of the phrase *planned obsolescence*. They didn't know that manufacturers made products *intending* that they break down or wear out very quickly so that people would be required to buy new ones. All consumers knew was that they were wasting a lot of money on useless goods. Things had not changed much since the nineteenth century. It was frustrating!

No one to turn to

There didn't seem to be anyone who cared about the problems of ordinary consumers, no one who could make the companies stop cheating the public.

President John F. Kennedy had campaigned on a platform that included a Consumer Bill of Rights. He said, "If consumers are offered inferior products, if prices are exorbitant, if drugs are unsafe or worthless, if the consumer is unable to choose on an informed basis, then his dollar is wasted, his health and safety may be threatened, and the national interest suffers." Kennedy's words were more politics than action, though. None of his promises to make business pay more attention to safety, honest advertising, quality, and a fair price seemed to be coming true.

There were a few isolated cases in which business was caught being recklessly irresponsible. A drug, thalidomide, was an example. Thalidomide had caused hundreds of severe birth defects in babies born to European women in 1962. Then a U.S. doctor named Frances Kelsey, of the Food and Drug Administration, uncovered the facts. Her investigation stopped the use of thalidomide in Europe. It also prevented a large drug manufacturer from selling the drug, a manufacturer who had been pressuring her to allow the sale of thalidomide in the United States.

The antitrust laws were another example. Senator Estes Kefauver exposed business combinations that set prices artificially high and then conspired to prevent anyone else from selling a similar product. But these were isolated cases, not the result of a strong, organized attack against unsafe products or unfair and dishonest practices.

People not only felt helpless about the inferior products they were stuck with, but also worried because garbage dumps were running out of room to hold all the junk they were throwing out. The more industry produced, the more raw natural resources it used, and the more waste products resulted.

The big cars used a lot of gas. When this gas was burned, it turned the air black with exhaust. The environment was becoming very polluted and dangerous to its inhabitants as a result of spending that had gotten out of control.

Upper: In 1962, Dr. Frances Kelsey urges the U.S. Senate to ban thalidomide because it caused birth defects.

Lower: Freddie Astbury, age 13, whose birth defects resulted from thalidomide. The drug crippled 432 children in Europe before Kelsey's fight resulted in a worldwide ban of the drug.

It was time someone did something about it. In 1966, with the scandal at General Motors, that someone suddenly appeared to be Mr. Ralph Nader. And we have seen what he and his Raiders and PIRGs have been able to do since the investigations in 1966.

A life without luxuries

But to accomplish what he has, Nader has had to sacrifice his private life. Early in his career, he decided never to marry, and on one occasion, he called it "a cruel choice" because he remembers family life as a boy with such affection, and he loves children. He knew, though, that to put in the long hours that his work would inevitably demand of him, he would have to make this sacrifice.

He remembered how his father, Nathra, had been able to do so much on a local level even with a large family to support. But this was because Ralph's mother, Rose, had done most of the child care and housekeeping. Ralph knew he wanted to tackle national problems and maintain a schedule of up to six lectures a week. He didn't think he would have time for a family too, so he decided he would never marry and have children.

Ralph's living situation is something of a legend in Washington. He could have afforded a lovely home with fine furnishings. Instead, during the 1960s and 1970s, he stayed in an old brownstone in an unfashionable section of Washington, in one large room with a bath.

His furniture consisted of a bed with no footboard, a bureau, a desk, a typewriter, and a throw rug. Papers and books were strewn everywhere. A pay telephone in the hall was his one contact with the outside world, which he limited as much as possible during his scarce hours at home.

He lived in this building for many years following the publication of his book and, probably because of the controversial nature of his work, never gave anyone his exact address. His landlady charged him a tiny rent and hated to raise it because this rent had become a symbol of Nader's unusual commitment.

In the 1980s, he moved away from the old rooming house, before it was torn down, and into a

$200-a-month apartment nearby. By Washington standards, his rent is still incredibly cheap. He still doesn't tell anyone his exact address; even his close friends never get invited over.

Nader isn't much of a consumer in other ways, either. He has no personal indulgences as most people do. He doesn't even own a television. He had a Studebaker in 1949, but then he gave up his driver's license. More recently, he has acquired one and even drives a car once in a while but still refuses to buy one.

For years he wore a few baggy blue suits and had only one extra pair of black shoes. An old raincoat was his only protection from the cold, no hat or gloves. Lately his colleagues have noticed that he dresses a little better, but he still travels with the same old ripped plastic briefcase bulging with papers. Judging from his choppy hairstyle, some people think he even cuts his own hair.

Nader takes the hundreds of thousands of dollars he makes from his many activities and puts almost all of it back into running the Center. He allows himself only the barest minimum for rent and food, never goes out on dates, and has only an occasional drink. He doesn't smoke or have any hobbies or relaxing leisure pastimes because he never takes the time to have them. His only indulgence is that he eats two desserts whenever he gets the chance. Because of his simple tastes, Nader claims he is able to live on less than $11,000 a year.

Ralph does not crave material possessions or status symbols. Moreover, he does not want to support business by buying anything. He even feels slightly betrayed when an employee buys a car or the newest popular product.

He is suspicious of advertising and products whose only aim is to gratify the passing whim of the consumer. This is partially because he simply hates waste of any kind and partially because he has witnessed how business exploits consumers to make huge, and sometimes illegal, profits.

| SURGEON GENERAL'S WARNING: Quitting Smoking Now Greatly Reduces Serious Risks to Your Health. |

| SURGEON GENERAL'S WARNING: Cigarette Smoke Contains Carbon Monoxide. |

| SURGEON GENERAL'S WARNING: Smoking By Pregnant Women May Result in Fetal Injury, Premature Birth, And Low Birth Weight. |

| SURGEON GENERAL'S WARNING: Smoking Causes Lung Cancer, Heart Disease, Emphysema, And May Complicate Pregnancy. |

Pressure from consumer groups and doctors resulted in health warnings on American cigarette packages. Cigarette companies fought the requirement, fearing that consumers would reject their product. Other rulings prohibit selling tobacco products on television or radio.

Some consumers resent Ralph

Fighting for consumer rights and advocating moderate consumer behavior is his total passion, but

Edward M. Swartz, author of Toys That Kill, *displayed potentially dangerous toys before the U.S. Senate Commerce Committee in 1971.*

in many cases it makes him unpopular with the target of his attacks, sometimes, even consumers themselves. Some have told him they don't like to have to justify buying a television or eating a hot dog *if that's what they want to do.* After all, it's a free country.

Despite Ralph's influence on consumer awareness, a lot of people resent him for thinking that it is his job to set an example for them. While many people admire him for doing just that, others are angered by the way he lives. They feel that he's trying to show them up and tell them how to live.

Be less wasteful, he preaches. Be more aware of consumer hazards and be willing to do something about them. Many people don't like to hear that their comfortable lives support the wastefulness.

He makes them feel guilty because he lives so meagerly, according to his staunch principles. Yes, he wants them to feel guilty, guilty enough to change. Whether consumers love him or hate him, they know where Ralph Nader stands at all times: on their side. In 1971 and 1972, he was even named one of America's most admired men in a Gallup Poll.

Some business leaders resent Ralph

Nader also annoys some people in business. They claim they merely respond to consumer demand. They say no one *forces* people to buy a product they don't want. They say that if a product is dangerous or useless, consumers simply won't purchase it. After all, consumers are used to taking risks when they buy products. They know that's just the way things are.

The problem, according to Nader, is that too often consumers learn too late that a product is dangerous or useless. They've already spent their money. They've already been injured. Moreover, many consumers do not know about the old saying, "let the buyer beware." Why should they have to be wily and try to outsmart a business? Why can't business operate in good faith with its customers? It is wrong to make dangerous products when they can easily avoid it.

The problem isn't lazy consumers that account for so much tragedy and waste, says Ralph. It's secretive business that permits — even encourages — secrecy and waste while it looks the other way.

Ralph has exposed a number of secretive practices: how some businesses conspire to fix prices that gouge the consumer, how they use hazardous and dangerous materials even if they are banned, how they label products unclearly or deliberately use misleading packaging.

Ralph makes business people especially uncomfortable because they know that Ralph is not crusading for personal gain, but for public well-being. They remember that he does without everything but the basic necessities when he could actually afford to live more lavishly than most of them do.

Infuriated critics always look for some gap in Ralph's armor, some imperfection. When they realize he's sincere, his confidence about the rightness of his beliefs makes them either scornful or totally frustrated. People who are not doing the right thing are uncomfortable around someone who is.

No one with something to hide likes to be threatened with an investigation by Ralph. Whether they are illegally releasing toxins into rivers or selling unsanitary food, the name Ralph Nader makes them very nervous.

"I wasn't anti-business then, and I'm not anti-business now. I'm just pro-people."
Ralph Nader, quoted in Richard Curtis's Ralph Nader's Crusade

"Sure, a lot of people hate us. The liberals hate us because we steal their thunder. They talk big and do little. The corporate establishment hates us because we destroy their carefully groomed images. Even a lot of housewives hate us because we're always bugging people to leave their t.v. sets and crap games and get to work."
A Nader's Raider, quoted in Richard Curtis's Ralph Nader's Crusade

*Opposite: Ralph Nader
criticized the Food and
Drug Administration in
1988 for trying to kill a
rule that makes fruit juice
companies reveal the
amount of real juice in
their products. New York
State Attorney General
Robert Abrams looks on.*

They know that no matter how loudly they deny
any wrongdoing, he and his staff will still investigate
them and expose their faults to the public. That's why
Ralph doesn't let his critics upset him. He knows he
has to continue investigating in order to protect the
public from crimes like these.

Raiders meet his standards

In the beginning, too, it was not easy for the Raiders
to follow the example of a man like Nader. For one
thing, he was almost never at the Center and he almost
never told anyone where he was. He was always
traveling, giving speeches about consumer advocacy
to keep money coming in to the Center.

His staff knew they couldn't count on Ralph to be
there if they needed him. It was useless to leave a
phone message for him since he almost never
answered his phone messages. If a problem with an
investigation arose, people at the Center usually had
to solve it on their own.

When Ralph was there, he seemed uncomfortable
interacting with people. He talked only about work
and avoided getting personal. He would hole up in his
office for eighteen hours a day, forever writing or
reading. It struck many people as strange that a man
so concerned with the health and safety of others
could be so hard to get close to. They did not yet
realize that while some people focus on individual
people, others focus their energies on causes.

One Raider remarked that the staff wanted to see
Ralph more often. They needed his leadership and
wanted the good feelings that come from working on
a team with a leader who is a friend as well as a guide.
Learning this, Nader was baffled. If they had the
freedom to pursue their own work, why would they
want time with him?

Working for Ralph Nader

The irony of working at the Center, where Raiders
investigate occupational health and safety, is that
Nader doesn't see his employees' uncomfortable
working conditions. But Raiders now know what
they are in for when they hire on with Ralph. Being
selfless is a normal part of public-interest work.

Rulings now require warning labels like this one for a common medication. Before consumer advocates like Nader demanded such labels on packages, people were often injured or killed using products improperly.

Caution: Do not give to children under 12 years of age or use for more than 10 days unless directed by a physician. **WARNINGS: AS WITH ANY DRUG, IF YOU ARE PREGNANT OR NURSING A BABY, SEEK THE ADVICE OF A HEALTH PROFESSIONAL BEFORE USING THIS PRODUCT. KEEP THIS AND ALL DRUGS OUT OF REACH OF CHILDREN. IN CASE OF ACCIDENTAL OVERDOSE SEEK PROFESSIONAL ASSISTANCE OR CONTACT A POISON CONTROL CENTER IMMEDIATELY.**

Ralph knows the Raiders will work for such low salaries and in such stressful surroundings because they believe in the cause as much as he does. They know he'll call in the middle of the night to talk about work, as he often does. They just pick up the receiver and say "Hello, Ralph." To work for Ralph is to work all the time.

He manages his staff with one simple principle: that he will never ask them to do anything that he himself will not do. In theory this sounds reasonable, but some people might say Nader does not live the life of a reasonable man. He does without sleep and without food. He travels constantly, he practically lives in airports, and he is almost never on time.

He never vacations and always works on weekends. He stays up through the night reading dry congressional reports and industry statistics so he can be armed with the facts. No, indeed, following Ralph Nader's example is no easy job.

Yet he has loyal colleagues, people who take their mission seriously. Ralph demands their complete loyalty and just about all their energy. They feel slightly guilty if they take a sunny Saturday off to be with their kids while Ralph slaves away at the office.

They have learned that Ralph views personal relationships and worldly possessions as almost irrelevant, that they have to adopt this same attitude if they want to work for Ralph. As hard as it often seems, they have to be as obsessed as he is.

More often than not, the Raiders simply don't take Saturday off. For the time that they work with Nader, most marry the job, just as Ralph has.

"Dear Ralph Nader..."

Although Ralph Nader has some critics, he has found that most citizens don't need much encouragement to speak out for their rights. This is proven by the huge volume of mail he receives from ordinary people complaining about products or companies and demanding that he investigate them.

The public outcry even serves as an informal survey for Ralph Nader. Ralph's consumer groups study the thousands of letters he receives. From the letters, they can spot troubling trends and potentially hazardous products. Literally thousands of consumer cases have come to light in this way.

Ralph has become familiar with the anger of the letter writers. He shares their anger and tries to act on it. In each case, the letters speak of financial and physical suffering.

Mental stress caused by their problems is also common. Some letters merely express annoyance, while some shed light on unbearable conditions or illegal activities. Many writers even offer to join the Raiders, so deep is their frustration.

Cries for help

Claire Nader, Ralph's sister and an anthropologist, is interested in the effects of stress on consumers. As part of a study, she compiled letters that people wrote to her brother in her book, *No Access to Law: Alternatives to the American Judicial System*. The letters reveal America's frustration with workmanship and the hope that Nader can improve the situation. "Oh, Mr. Nader," writes one person, "they cheat like the devil himself — all of them. How many times have I bought boiled ham in a cellophane wrapping, only to find when I lifted up the top two slices, the rest was bits and pieces heavily laced with fat."

"Dear Mr. Nader," laments another, "Every cake I baked, it only half rose in the oven, then when I took it out, the rest of it flopped! I hate it, I hate it, I hate it! My pigs in the blankets get burned on top and bottom and the inside is raw. I have been embarrassed too many times, and apologized too many times, that I'm a nervous wreck from this stove."

"Dear Ralph Nader," another writes, "I was so glad to read you are investigating the medical profession. It would be impossible for me to describe what I've undergone for 8 years due to a wrong medical diagnosis, and a sloppy operation, performed by an unqualified surgeon. I've lost piles of money considering what I've spent in medical fees and not being able to work. So this terrible operation, which I didn't need in the first place, has cost me a normal life, and exposed me to the largest group of racketeers in existence — the doctors."

"Dear Ralph Nader, I find myself in an intolerable

"One day we walked into a little food mart and got a popsicle and my friend Tom said his tasted funny. So I said lets get your money back. So we went back and said we wished to get our money back or we would write to Ralph Nader. So he said go ahead. So we are writing you. Mike."
From letter to Nader, quoted in Robert Buckhorn's Nader, the People's Lawyer

position, that of being forced to pay outrageously high medical coverage for neglect, indifference and costly carelessness while hospitalized."

"Dear Mr. Nader, The things I could tell you about [a state institution for people who are retarded] would make your hair stand straight up. They brought [my son] out to us with two swollen black eyes, bruises of a man's fist covering his body, with cigarette burns on the bottoms of his feet. Please investigate and make a loud noise about the whole thing."

Thoroughly disgusted

"Ralph Nader, Bless your heart for being a crusader and trying to help the underdog [get] a break. My husband and I are 79 and 80 years old. We need all kinds of medication. I shouldn't have to fret that after I've saved for my old age I should have to dish it all out to the blood suckers. Get after the doctors and drugs, etc."

"Dear Ralph, We gave a lot of money for this refrigerator and it isn't worth it. We thought we were buying a good product. The repairman has been out four or five times and I am thoroughly disgusted."

"Dear Ralph Nader, When so many people seem to want to avoid certain additives — chemicals, sugar, preservatives — why must we be forced to use foods containing these additives. I cannot take the time to read all the ingredients listed, nor do I understand the chemicals involved. Is anything being done to eliminate this constant use of hazardous additives in our food?"

"Dear Mr. Nader, Why does everyone ignore the rip-offs the retired people are getting who live in mobile home parks? Park owners get a profit. We get cheap sinks, cheap faucets, knobs that you can't grip, windows that won't open, doors that won't close, gouged linoleum. Under warranty? Yes, when you pay for it."

Learning to think like Nader

Just from this small sample of letters, it is plain to Ralph Nader that consumers everywhere are being victimized. They are suffering intolerably as a result of dishonest businesses and dangerous products.

Nader can't respond to each letter personally, although each one makes him more determined to stop customers from being taken advantage of. But he investigates many of the activities that result in the kind of suffering voiced by the letter writers. Doing this, he hopes he can make the system of business and government take responsibility for their mistakes.

Remembering how his mother always encouraged him to stop complaining and do something about a problem, Ralph developed a way of looking at things that helped him begin to question shoddy design and threats to safety. In short, he questions *everything*.

"Take, for instance, the front bumper of an automobile," says Ralph. "Nearly every day most people casually look at car bumpers. Their view usually stops there. A few moments of consumer education would open the following sequence:

"Bumpers are supposed to protect automobiles from minor damage in minor collisions. For many years, however, bumper design has been largely ornamental. Much needless damage has resulted when cars bumped or crashed at two, three, five or eight miles an hour. Such damage costs motorists over one billion dollars a year. Insurance premiums rise as a consequence. More replacement parts have

"Basically [my] motivation is simply this. When I see people decapitated, crushed, bloodied, and broken, and that is what we are really talking about in auto safety, the fatalities and horrible carnage involved, I ask myself what can the genius of man do to avoid it?"

Ralph Nader, quoted in
Robert Buckhorn's
Nader, the People's Lawyer

Poisonous chemicals spew from a smokestack in Pennsylvania and return to earth in the form of acid rain, killing forests and wildlife, even corroding cars and buildings. Factories claim pollution control is too costly. Meanwhile, consumers feel the costs of pollution in medical and repair bills.

Because of investigations by Nader and other public citizens, nursing homes now regulate themselves more strictly and must report to regulatory agencies. Care of the elderly is a national issue, and conditions are improving as alert citizens expose abuses.

"[There are] major fire disasters, fatal food contamination, corporate manipulations, drug experimentation beyond proper medical discretion, kickbacks in drug sales for residents, abysmal lack of medical supervision, and strong evidence that such abuses are more epidemic than episodic."

Ralph Nader, in his
investigation of nursing
home conditions, quoted
in Richard Curtis's
Ralph Nader's Crusade

to be produced. More coal, steel, glass, plastic and other raw materials must be used, and more fuel expended. Prices of these commodities mount. Pollution of air and water increases.

"What consumers spend on bumper repair," concludes Nader, "they do not spend on other goods and services which they might otherwise have purchased. Why did the auto companies design such bumpers? Could it be the companies profited by faulty design and covered their actions by promoting the [looks] of egg-shell bumpers?"

The investigations

Ralph's dogged determination in exposing faulty car production is what made him famous. Yet he has been responsible for far more than changes in car design.

Some of the more important reports that he and his Raiders have produced, among scores of them, are

• *The Chemical Feast*, an investigation into the Food and Drug Administration's lazy enforcement of banned additives in food;

• *The Vanishing Air*, a report on the shocking truth about air pollution, and how industries will fully ignore laws designed to stop them from sending deadly chemicals into the air, water, and soil;

• *Old Age: The Last Segregation*, about the disgusting and tragic conditions in homes for the elderly;

• *Who Runs Congress?*, an inside look at the way the people's representatives are influenced by big-business lobbies and pressure from government agencies to pass laws favorable to them;

• *Bitter Wages: Disease and Injury on the Job*, which shows how employers often ignore dangerous, even deadly, working conditions and the suffering of workers injured because of hazardous work places.

There are many, many more reports. All expose some terrible secret. All name the names of those responsible for keeping the secrets from the public and blame them for deliberately misleading the public so that they might profit from the people's ignorance.

Reports get noticed

The reports immediately awaken the public to problems they don't know exist. An eager news media widely publishes the details of Ralph's discoveries, and a previously quiet public demands action to correct the problem.

Perhaps it is one of Ralph's shortcomings, his critics say, that he does not stay on one subject long enough to see radical change take place. The number of issues he and his Raiders investigate is overwhelming — land use; unsafe toys; antitrust laws; x-ray exposure; housing abuses; banking power; medical services; the U.S. Congress; pension discrimination; false advertising; veterans' affairs; women's issues; insurance fraud; lethal pesticides; and the national forests. And this is only a partial list!

There is more — the paper industry; antibiotics in meats; alcohol and narcotics; gasoline octane ratings; white-collar crime; flammable children's clothing; the American Automobile Association; air and water pollution; cancer-causing food additives; occupational safety standards; additives in baby food; tire and rubber manufacturing; the mental health establishment; corporate regulation and competition; the beef, poultry, and pork industries; airplane safety standards and unfair air fares; coal-mining occupational hazards and health benefits for miners; and nursing home conditions and abuse of the elderly. Is there an area of American life that Nader and his staff have missed? It seems not.

Many critics use Ralph's habit of investigating many different subjects to blame him for not really

"The cosmetic treatment of food covers up the stripping of nutrients. Coloring, preservatives, seasonings, and tenderizers camouflage the fat content in frankfurters, their decrease in meat protein, and the substandard quality of the meat. The emphasis on snacks, chemically doused bakery goods, and soft drinks have a serious effect on young people's food habits and nutrition. Millions grow up watching television believing that Pepsi-Cola and Coca-Cola provide health and vigor. Small wonder then that the Department of Agriculture shows a decline in nutritional adequacy of American diets."
Ralph Nader, quoted in
Richard Curtis's
Ralph Nader's Crusade

doing anything about the problems he uncovers. They see him as a nosy lawyer who just wants to expose their secrets and get them in trouble.

Ralph, though, has proven that his method of simply exposing the problems works. It gets attention and raises the awareness of the public that problems exist. Today, hundreds of consumer organizations actively try to change laws to protect the consumer.

Setting a trend

Many of these changes happened because of Nader's investigations. Many more happened because people followed his example and spoke out when they saw a problem. Hundreds of consumer problems remain, but it was Ralph Nader's influence and awareness that started the consumer revolution.

When he became one of the nation's most vocal consumer advocates, he faced the task of educating consumers about things that were being kept secret from them. He knew that no reforms could happen until people knew just how badly they were needed. He became a crusader for public health and safety, but he knew he couldn't do it alone. He needed the total support of the people. They would have to demand change too and work for change together. Thus, part of his program has been to create public citizens.

The more he crusaded, the more people's awareness grew. They formed literally hundreds of consumer organizations of their own. They pressured their lawmakers to vote on issues that were important to them. Many new laws protecting the consumer were passed in this way.

Even with the new laws, though, many unsafe products and practices still exist because it costs so much money to enforce safety rules.

Pollution: a consumer issue

Ralph and his Raiders have worked hard on exposing perhaps the worst secret of all: industrial pollution of the environment. Ralph calls pollution "compulsory consumption," because the public has been forced to breathe the foul air and drink the poisoned water that industries give off. Thus, he thinks of pollution as an important consumer issue.

Some business leaders claim they try to save the consumer money by not adding the costs of pollution control and safety research to their products. They insist that preventing pollution would cause expenses consumers would be unwilling to pay for.

Ralph has dedicated his life to exposing these claims as myths. Industry created these stories to hide wasteful, dangerous practices, says Ralph.

Industries save themselves money, he discovered, when they just dump their toxic wastes into rivers and lakes, rather than store it in safe containers. They save themselves money by letting poisonous gas belch from their smokestacks instead of putting in pollution-control equipment.

Industry, says Ralph, doesn't tell if it leaks hazardous chemicals because it doesn't want to face public disapproval. Nor does it want to take on the cost of cleaning up a mess or of providing health care that might be necessary when people become sick from the pollution.

One of the more dangerous polluters, says Nader, is the nuclear industry, which is careless about radioactive wastes. These wastes cause cancer in humans, yet Ralph has discovered nuclear plants and nuclear regulating agencies that are reluctant to tell the public that they have been exposed to radiation — and how much radiation.

The cooling towers of the Three Mile Island nuclear power plant, site of the worst nuclear accident in U.S. history, loom over farmer Claire Nissley's field as he harvests crops. The badly regulated nuclear energy industry remains one of Ralph Nader's primary targets.

"Open your window and take a deep breath. You'll feel lousy."
A print advertisement of the 1960s, protesting air pollution, quoted in Richard Curtis's Ralph Nader's Crusade

"Some of us like the smell. It smells like money."
William Halladay, of Atlantic-Richfield Oil Co., about the foul odor coming from a refinery, quoted in Nader's The Consumer and Corporate Accountability

*Ralph Nader once called
hot dogs "America's most
dangerous unguided
missiles" because they
were thirty percent fat.
Today, hot dogs may have
fifteen percent fat at most,
and meat packers must list
their ingredients, including
chemical preservatives,
on the package.*

Ralph believes it is the duty of industry that produces toxic wastes to pay the cleanup bills. It shouldn't pass on costs to the consumer. After all, he says, it's everyone's air, water, soil, and health that they're violating, not just their own. It might be expensive at first to put in pollution controls, but Ralph doesn't think business should put expense ahead of public health.

Quality of life

It is impossible to calculate the number of lives that have been safeguarded because of Ralph Nader's career as a professional watchdog. It is possible to see the kinds of improvements that have been made because of his vigilance and the consumer awareness he has inspired in others.

Cars are now recalled by their makers and safety defects are repaired. Some car manufacturers are even so confident about the quality of their product that they try to out-compete each other now to see who can give the customer a better warranty. Cars now have standard safety features, such as seat belts and safety glass, and some have air bags.

Hot dogs now have a maximum of fifteen percent fat, rather than the thirty percent that many manufacturers used to put in their hot dogs — without telling consumers. Additives and ingredients in food must appear on the package label. And businesses must list nutritional contents on food packages as well as date the food for freshness.

Cigarette packages must carry plainly visible health warnings. Cigarette advertising is banned from television. Airplanes and many restaurants have non-smoking sections. There is even pressure to declare tobacco a drug, so that it will be regulated under drug safety standards.

X-rays taken in a physician's office must be taken by a trained technician, and both patient and technician must be protected from cancer-causing x-ray radiation by a lead apron.

Toys that have injured children have been removed from the market. Fabrics, especially those used in children's pajamas, must be made nonflammable.

Workers must have physical protection from dangerous chemicals and toxins. Advertising may not make false claims for a product's performance.

Drugs must be tested for safety and effectiveness before they are given to people.

Quieter years

The years since 1975 have been relatively quiet for Ralph Nader. Since he started the consumer revolution, many of his ideas are now accepted as common wisdom. He still gives lectures, although he only does thirty a year now instead of 150 a year. He's still active in consumer affairs, but the newspapers don't give him as much attention as they used to. Still, he remains a symbol of ordinary citizens who can right the wrongs inflicted on them by business and government by speaking up against them.

In 1986, the Nader family lost Ralph's older brother, Shafik. He died of cancer at home in Winsted, Connecticut. For the first time in over twenty years, Ralph stopped working and went to stay with his parents at home. He stayed with them for weeks, and when he returned to work, his co-workers thought he seemed quieter than usual.

"I have a very stable set of purposes and convictions. I know it is going to be a rocky road so I am not ruffled very easily. I am sort of programmed to anticipate all these things, and I try to do what I can to prepare myself. I don't get all clutched up or nervous if things go wrong. I have an inner consistency that carries me through."
Ralph Nader, quoted in Robert Buckhorn's Nader, the People's Lawyer

"There has been concern among a lot of consumer people that Ralph was overextending himself."
A member of the Carter administration, formerly a consumer advocate, quoted in U.S. News & World Report

Ralph had been doing a lot of thinking while he was gone. He still cared about safe consumer products and consumer activism, but he decided to put his energy into a few projects rather than try to tackle every problem at once. He thought he could make more of an impact this way.

But more adversity awaited him. Ralph became very sick with Bell's palsy. The disease froze the right side of his face and made it difficult for him to talk, eat, and even smile. The doctors told him it was caused, in part, by his stressful life. Ralph knew he had to slow down. Gradually, he recovered until his face twitched only a bit, but he kept out of the public eye for some time until he felt better.

What happened to Winsted

While he was in Winsted, Ralph noticed ominous changes in his hometown and became worried about its future. He noticed that a rich land developer had bought a lot of beautiful, wooded land in Winsted — almost a million dollars' worth — and was going to cut down all the trees and build condominiums.

The developer even wanted to tear down his own house, a historically important building dating back to the American Revolution. He said it was impractical!

The main street of Winsted, Connecticut, where Ralph Nader lived as a boy.

54

A giant mall was being built just outside of Winsted. What worried Ralph most wasn't just that congestion and ugliness were about to disrupt the peaceful life in his hometown, but that the townspeople didn't seem to be trying to stop the disruption.

After Shafik's death, Ralph felt even more attached to his town. He wanted to preserve the idyllic life that he remembered enjoying as a boy. So he and his sister, Claire, immediately organized the townspeople to protest the development. They hired a citizen activist named Ellen Thomas to live in Winsted and help the townspeople circulate petitions and put pressure on the local government to stop the tree cutting and condominium building. They hired a lawyer to fight the case in the local courts. Ralph was helping citizens to fight for their rights again.

To prevent land development in Winsted, Claire Nader joined forces with her famous brother.

Back in the national eye

In 1988, Ralph Nader suddenly returned to the national scene when he helped the citizens of California pass a referendum, or law by popular vote. The referendum was designed to make automobile insurance companies lower their rates.

Californians paid the highest car insurance rates in the country, sometimes thousands of dollars more than people in other parts of the country paid to get the same kind of insurance protection. They thought this was unfair and that the insurance companies were taking advantage of them.

Ralph sensed the citizens' unhappiness and saw the potential to make a public uprising out of the issue. For the first time in his life, he became involved in political campaigning. Fighting against him were insurance companies that spent $70 million to convince the voters to vote against the proposal. Nader gave talks. A group called Voter Revolt formed, led by former Nader's Raider Harvey Rosenfield. This group spent only $2 million, but it was able to rally the voters to pass the law lowering insurance rates.

A poll taken later showed that two-thirds of the California voters would have voted to pass Proposition 103 just because Ralph Nader's name was associated with the cause. He was back in the forefront of citizen activism.

"My father taught me a long time ago that the highest thing after attaining a measure of progress or success is to be able to endure it. That is what I always counsel the students. Don't let that ego get in your way. Don't start getting a swollen head. Keep your eye on the objective and work harder, and harder, and harder."
Ralph Nader, quoted in Robert Buckhorn's Nader, the People's Lawyer

From apples to congressional raises

Ralph worked hard in 1988 on a number of other causes of national interest. He worked to stop apple farmers from using a chemical pesticide, Alar, on their crops. The Food and Drug Administration had discovered that Alar caused a high rate of cancer in children. The public outcry over the dangerous chemical resulted in a government ban on the use of Alar on food crops.

Ralph also fought Congress when it wanted to give each member of the Senate and House a high pay raise. Again, Ralph sensed the citizens' anger. The government already spent more money than it had. The national budget deficit was hundreds of billions of dollars. Besides, the minimum wage for workers was only $3.25 an hour, barely enough to live on, and Congress hadn't raised that wage in almost ten years!

Again, Ralph spoke out. He told members of Congress that giving themselves a pay raise was outrageous. He said that they should be able to live on the $89,500 a year they already received. He said they should do their jobs just for the honor of serving democracy. He added that a big part of the job's reward was the power, not the money, it gave them. The media paid a lot of attention to Ralph. Congress watched as the majority of citizens openly agreed with him.

Seeing how unpopular a raise would make them, the members of Congress voted against giving themselves a pay raise — only to ignore public opinion and Nader's arguments in late 1989. In November, Congress pushed its raises through, raises of $8,900 to $20,000 a year each. At the same time, Congress decided perhaps it could raise the minimum wage — by 1990, workers will start at a minimum $3.80 an hour and by 1991, at $4.25 an hour.

The future through Ralph's eyes

Nader has renewed his commitment to inspiring citizen activism on the local level, where effective changes can be made. He would like to see people getting involved in local problems, trying to make life better for the community rather than waiting for their government to fix the problems.

"Patriotism begins at home. Love of country in fact is inseparable from citizen action to make the country more lovable. This means working to end poverty, discrimination, corruption, greed and other conditions that weaken the promise and potential of America. Citizenship as an obligation of patriotism is a purifier of its misuses."
Ralph Nader, Life, July 1971

Nader also believes group action will be the way to solve consumer problems in the future, problems such as poor service or the high cost of energy.

Two examples of this group approach have already saved money for many consumers. In New York, eighty-five heating-oil buyers formed a syndicate, or association, to buy their fuel at a discount bulk rate. In Wisconsin, 85,000 electricity consumers paid $5 each to join a watchdog Citizens' Utility Board. The board pushed for rules that forced the power companies to lower the electric rates and set up energy conservation programs.

"Consumers should be assertive enough to turn their economy into a buyer's market," says Nader. In other words, they should make the market respond to them and not let big business tell them what to do.

Why we need Ralph Nader

Ralph will be remembered for raising consumer awareness in a general way, not for any specific victory. To be remembered in this way has taken thirty years of methodical and persistent crusading.

He has changed the way consumers look at what they buy. He has showed America that it is legitimate to protest corporate dishonesty. He has shown Americans how to protest, and many have followed his example.

Ralph has shown consumers the link between corporate selfishness and indifference to consumers. He has shown that government remains badly prepared to fight corporate greed, and perhaps this is his most important contribution.

Today, the public is more willing than ever to demand action when it sees corporate neglect damaging their lives. The public is more aware of the power of its collective voice to sway elected officials. Corporations and politicians now know they will have to answer to an increasingly skeptical public.

Ralph has always had an optimist's pure belief in the perfectibility of our system. He has passed this passion on to the public. "It's your system," he has persistently maintained. "It's up to you to make it work better."

The country has changed. Ironically, the success

"How do you get people to become serious about deciding things for themselves instead of letting other people decide things for them?"
Ralph Nader, quoted in
Rolling Stone

"I think he started something that has become much larger than he is. While he is still an important part of it, the consumer movement has in fact grown larger than Ralph."
Carole Tucker Foreman,
Assistant Secretary of
Agriculture for the Carter
administration, quoted in
U.S. News & World Report

Opposite: Many of the revolutionary things Ralph Nader believed as an early consumer advocate are common wisdom now. People are now more aware of food additives and the safety of their homes, cars, and work places. More and more are willing to become public citizens, too, eagerly voicing their concerns and protecting their rights as consumers.

of Ralph's reform movement has grown to the point that the country doesn't really need Ralph to show it what to do. He has become a symbol for citizens who have started hundreds of independent consumer action groups. He has been a success at getting across the message that people count.

Public Interest Research Groups (PIRGs)

In the early 1970s, using some of the $425,000 he received from General Motors, Ralph Nader started the Public Interest Research Group, which investigates issues that are of interest to consumers and students. Listed below are states with local PIRGs and their addresses:

Alaska: P.O. Box 1093, Anchorage 99510
California: 1660 Corinth Ave., West Los Angeles 90025
Colorado: 1724 Gilpin St., Denver 80218
Connecticut: University of Connecticut, Box U-8, Storrs 06268
Florida: 1441 E. Fletcher Ave., No. 2200-3, Tampa 33612
Indiana: Indiana Memorial Union, Bloomington 47405
Iowa: Iowa State University, Memorial Union, Room 36, Ames 50011
Maine: 92 Bedford St., Portland 04103
Maryland: University of Maryland, 3110 Main Dining Hall, College Park 20742
Massachusetts: 29 Temple Pl., Boston 02111
Michigan: 220 N. Chestnut St., Lansing 48933
Minnesota: 2412 University Ave. SE, Minneapolis 55414
Missouri: 4144 Lindell Blvd., Suite 219, St. Louis 63108
Montana: 356 Corbin Hall, Missoula 59812
New Jersey: 84 Paterson St., New Brunswick 08901
New Mexico: University of New Mexico, Box 66 SUB, Albuquerque 87131
New York: 9 Murray St., New York City 10007
Ohio: Oberlin College, Wilder Hall, Box 25, Oberlin 44074
Oregon: 27 S.W. Arthur St., Portland 97201
Rhode Island: 228 Weybosset St., Providence 02903
Vermont: 43 State St., Montpelier 05602
Washington: 5628 University Way NE, Seattle 98105
West Virginia: West Virginia University, Mountainlair SOW, Morgantown 26506
Wisconsin: 520 University Ave., Madison 53703

For More Information . . .

Organizations

The following organizations can provide information about consumer rights, about laws designed to protect the consumer, about environmental concerns of interest to the consumer, and about mismanagement in government. Write to them if you would like to know more about issues of interest to you. Many of them operate on tight budgets, so enclose a stamped envelope with your name and address written on it that they can use when they respond to you. In your letter, be sure to tell them exactly what you want to know, and include your name, address, and age.

Americans for Democratic Action
1511 K Street NW, Suite 941
Washington, DC 20005

Center for the Study of Responsive
    Law
P.O. Box 19367
Washington, DC 20036

Citizens Against Government Waste
1511 K Street NW, Suite 643
Washington, DC 20005

Consumer Education and Protective
    Association International
6048 Ogontz Avenue
Philadelphia, PA 19141

Public Information Center
U.S. Environmental Protection
    Agency (EPA)
401 M Street SW
Washington, DC 20460

Public Citizen
P.O. Box 19404
Washington, DC 20036

*For U.S. government pamphlets
for consumers . . .*
Consumer Information Center
Pueblo, CO 81009

*For queries about consumer
protection, food, drugs, cosmetics,
medicines, and electronics . . .*
Food and Drug Administration
Office of Consumer Affairs
5600 Fishers Lane, Room 16-63
Rockville, MD 20857

*For queries about government ethics
and reform issues . . .*
Common Cause
2030 M Street NW
Washington, DC 20036

For a free catalogue . . .
U.S. Consumer Product Safety Commission
Washington, DC 20207

Books and Articles

By Ralph Nader —

"The Profits in Pollution," *The Progressive*. April 1970.
"Safety on the Job," *The New Republic*. June 15, 1968.
"Seven Safety Features Cars Need Most," *Science Digest*. August 1966.
Unsafe at Any Speed. (Grossman)
"We Need a New Kind of Patriotism," *Life*. July 9, 1971.

About Ralph Nader —

"The Aging of Ralph Nader," *Newsweek*. December 16, 1985.
Nader and the Power of Everyman. Gorey (Grosset & Dunlap)
Nader: The People's Lawyer. Buckhorn (Prentice Hall)
"Ralph Nader: Building a New Empire With More Activists, More Money, and Less
    Media Attention," *Parade*. May 23, 1982.
Ralph Nader Presents More Action for a Change. Griffin (Dembner)
"Ralph Nader: The Rolling Stone Interview," *Rolling Stone*. November 1975. Joe Klein.
Ralph Nader's Crusade. Curtis (Macrae Smith)

About Consumer Issues —

The Chemical Feast. Turner (Grossman)
Enough! The Revolt of the American Consumer. Faber (Farrar, Straus & Giroux)
The Hidden Persuaders. Packard (McKay)
Hot War on the Consumer. Sanford (Pitman)
The Jungle. Sinclair (Harper & Row)
Silent Spring. Carson (Houghton Mifflin)
Toys That Kill. Swartz (Random House)
200,000,000 Guinea Pigs: New Dangers in Everyday Foods, Drugs and Cosmetics.
    Fuller (Putnam)
The Vanishing Air. Esposito (Grossman)

Glossary

accountability
Being answerable for one's words and actions, and for the consequences of those words and actions. Nader's reform movement aimed to make industry have full accountability to the consumer, to explain its actions, especially if it harms, cheats, or endangers the consumer.

additives
Substances added to something to improve, strengthen, or otherwise alter it. Additives in food improve taste and shelf life of food, but many are unnecessary and unsafe for humans.

antitrust
A term that describes laws and efforts to regulate businesses to prevent them from having an unfair advantage in the marketplace.

barter
The practice of trading goods and services without exchanging money. Before standardized money existed, barter was a common form of exchange.

boycotting
Undermining a business by refusing to buy a product or otherwise deal with it.

bureaucracy
A government or administrative body that follows such inflexible rules of operation that it often cannot proceed with effective action. Such an agency or other body

usually spreads its power and authority over many offices so that no one person in the organization is responsible for the whole.

compulsory consumption
Any form of consumption that the consumer cannot avoid, such as environmental pollution. Nader believes that the public is forced to consume industrial pollution against its will because it is exposed to it.

corporation
Any group of people legally united into one organization with rights, privileges, and obligations that are distinct from those of its individual members. A typical corporation is usually a business operated by many people for the profit of shareholders in the company.

Corvair
The sports car designed and produced by General Motors from 1959 to 1969 and the center of Nader's argument that American car makers sacrificed safety for sporty looks and higher sales.

DDT
A colorless insecticide harmful to humans and animals when swallowed or absorbed through the skin. DDT was widely used to spray crops and trees to prevent insect damage until Rachel Carson's *Silent Spring* exposed its dangers to humans. DDT was subsequently banned in the United States.

fraud
A deception deliberately practiced in order to profit unfairly. For years, some advertisers made grandiose claims about their products in order to boost sales.

free enterprise
An economic system in which private business operates in competition with other businesses for profit and with very little government regulation.

Gallup Poll
A survey of public opinion; George Horace Gallup founded the American Institute of Public Opinion, which collects statistics on people's attitudes on various issues.

grass-roots
A term describing social or political movements originating with ordinary citizens, whether alone or in small groups, rather than from large institutions.

Great Depression
The period between the stock market crash of October 1929 and 1941 when the United States and many other industrial countries experienced tremendous economic upheaval. Banks and businesses failed, and millions were thrown into poverty.

harassment
Systematically threatening, persecuting, or bothering someone in order to cause mental harm.

Industrial Revolution
The period from the late 1700s through the early twentieth century when the economy shifted away from agriculture to industries. People began to produce large

numbers of items in factories and sell them worldwide rather than produce handmade items to be sold locally.

monopoly
Any entity that has exclusive possession or control of a commercial activity and can thereby limit consumer choice. Because it has no competition, the monopoly can charge whatever it wants for the product or service.

occupational safety
Safety on the job. Employers must inform their employees about and protect them from dangerous chemicals, machinery, and other hazards in the work place.

ombudsman
A government official who investigates citizens' complaints against the government.

planned obsolescence
The practice of designing and manufacturing a product so it wears out or becomes obsolete, thereby forcing consumers to replace it.

public citizen
A term used by Nader to describe any resident of any country who actively participates in making the country's system of government and business serve the interests of the public, and not just its own selfish interests.

public-interest issues
Issues that affect the life, health, and well-being of the general public. For example, the pollution of the environment is a matter of public interest.

service economy
An economy based on providing information and services to consumers rather than on manufacturing. In the last half of the twentieth century, as it has become cheaper for businesses to produce goods abroad, many factories closed in the United States. So many Americans began providing services — including anything from teaching to selling insurance to doing laundry to working in a restaurant to repairing goods.

syndicate
An association of people formed to carry out an enterprise.

thalidomide
A sedative drug removed from sale because it caused severe birth defects.

toxic waste
Any poisonous by-product of industrial or nuclear production (whether liquid, solid, or gas); its release into the environment can cause death and disease in living things.

truth in advertising
A policy begun by the Federal Trade Commission, stating that businesses may not make false claims for products in their advertisements.

warranty
A guarantee from a seller that the buyer will be protected in the event that the product breaks or malfunctions. New car buyers usually receive a warranty for free repairs or replacement for the first few years they own their cars.

whistle blowing
> Nader's policy of keeping business and government honest by urging employees to report any dangerous or illegal practices by their employers.

white-collar crime
> Any nonviolent crime that deliberately defrauds, cheats, or endangers the public interest; it is so named because the criminals who commit white-collar crime usually hold "respectable" jobs but then abuse the power of those jobs for personal gain at the expense of the public.

Chronology

1865 The American Civil War increases demand for uniforms. Men's ready-made clothing industry is created. Ready-made consumer goods become popular.

1880s The Industrial Revolution increases production of consumer goods. No laws exist to protect consumers of these goods.

1883 Dr. Harvey W. Wiley notices chemical additives in food and argues unsuccessfully for a pure food law.

1890s Wiley speaks out publicly for removal of impurities and additives from food.

1900-14 Reform movements, including the consumer movement, become popular in the United States. This period is called the Progressive Era.

1902 Wiley conducts experiment with food additives to see effect on human health. He publishes "The Poison Squad." Public uproar follows.

1906 **February** — Upton Sinclair publishes *The Jungle*; it describes the filthy and unsanitary conditions of meat-packing plants.
June — Public outrage over *The Jungle* moves Congress to pass Pure Food and Drug Act. The law, however, does not list impurities to be banned.

1908 **February** — Robert N. Harper is first person convicted of violating Pure Food and Drug Act; he misleads the public about his product, Brane-Fude.

1912 The Association of Advertising Clubs of America founds Better Business Bureau to devise a code of business ethics and discourage advertising fraud. Nathra and Rose Nader immigrate from their native Lebanon to rural Winsted, Connecticut, with their eldest son, Shafik.

1914 Federal Trade Commission is created to ensure fair competition among businesses, to regulate against monopolies, and to monitor the advertising industry for fraudulent practices.
World War I begins and lasts until 1918. After the war, Americans become a nation of consumers.

1929 **October** — The Great Depression begins: the New York Stock Exchange crashes; factories and banks fail; eventually millions are out of work.

1930 Wiley, "Father of the Pure Food Law," dies at age 85.

1933 F. J. Schlink and Arthur Kallet, leaders of Consumers' Research, publish

100,000 Guinea Pigs: Dangers in Everyday Foods, Drugs and Cosmetics, detailing abuses committed despite the Pure Food and Drug Act.

1934 **February 27** — Ralph Nader is born to Nathra and Rose Nader.

1938 **June 25** — Despite business opposition, Food, Drug, and Cosmetic Act passes suddenly because of 107 deaths resulting from a harmful drug.

1941 **December 7** — America enters World War II. Food, fuel, and consumer goods become scarce as industry produces military equipment.

1945 **August 14** — War ends. Americans begin era of huge consumer spending to make up for war shortages. Unprecedented numbers of children are born in postwar rebuilding. Consuming becomes American pastime.

1951 Ralph Nader enters Princeton University.

1952 *Consumer Reports* subscriptions reach one-half million.

1953 The Flammable Fabrics Act passes, requiring that all children's pajamas be made of material that does not easily catch fire.

1955 Ralph Nader enters Harvard Law School.

1957 Publication of *The Hidden Persuaders* by Vance Packard uncovers how advertising industry uses psychological techniques to get consumers to buy products. Revival of consumer movement begins. Senator Estes Kefauver exposes suspect business practices in pharmaceutical industry.

1958 Nader's "American Cars: Designed for Death," his first published article, appears in the *Harvard Law School Record.*

1959 General Motors puts dangerous Corvair car on the market. Nader, now in U.S. Army, buys four dozen pairs of socks at post exchange (PX) when he is stationed in New Jersey.

1960 Senator John F. Kennedy successfully campaigns for the presidency on promises to become the consumers' lobbyist.

1961 Dr. Frances Kelsey finds that a drug, thalidomide, causes severe birth defects. Governments remove drug from market in Europe and prevent its being sold in the United States. President Kennedy awards Kelsey a medal for distinguished public service.

1962 **March** — Kennedy announces Consumer Bill of Rights to Congress. Rachel Carson's *Silent Spring* exposes damages caused by pesticide spraying.

1963 Nader presents ombudsman bill to Connecticut state legislature. It fails.

1964 Nader moves to Washington, D.C., to work for Daniel Patrick Moynihan at the U.S. Department of Labor. He soon leaves department to write full-time.

1965 **November** — Nader publishes *Unsafe at Any Speed*; it exposes fatal design of some automobiles and demands that automakers pay attention to safety.

General Motors Corporation hires detectives to investigate Nader's private life, hoping to damage his public image.

1966   **February** — Nader testifies before Congress on automobile safety.
March — James Roche, chairman of General Motors, publicly apologizes to Nader for the illegal investigation of his private life.
Newsweek runs story about Nader on March 21. He becomes household word.
June — Nader sues General Motors for invasion of privacy, winning a $425,000 settlement.
Traffic and Motor Vehicle Safety Act becomes law.

1967   The Flammable Fabrics Act is amended to include home furnishings, shoes, and hats, and to set higher standards for protection.
Wholesome Meat Act passes due to direct involvement of Nader.
Meat Inspection Act passes, demanding cleanliness and inspection standards for meat produced and sold within a state.

1968   Wholesome Poultry Products Act, Natural Gas Pipeline Safety Act, and Radiation Control for Health and Safety Act pass due to efforts of Nader.

1969   **May** — Nader establishes Center for the Study of Responsive Law (CSRL) in Washington, D.C., to fight for the public interest.
Coal Mine Health and Safety Act passes, partially due to Nader.
Nader's socks, purchased at the PX in 1959, finally wear out.

1970   Nader establishes the Public Interest Research Group (PIRG), a law firm resulting in a network of student organizations fighting for local issues.
Public Health Cigarette Smoking Act passes, demanding health warnings on all cigarette packaging and advertising.
Federal Hazardous Substances Act passes, giving the Food and Drug Administration (FDA) the authority to ban or control sale or promotion of toxic or hazardous substances.
Despite Flammable Fabrics Act, loopholes in the law contribute to 250,000 injuries and 4,000 deaths from burning clothing or fabric.
Occupational Health and Safety Act passes after research by Ralph Nader.
Consumer Reports subscriptions top two million.
CSRL publishes *The Chemical Feast*, by James Turner, its first influential report. Another report, *The Vanishing Air*, soon follows.

1971   Ralph Nader is named to the Gallup Poll's "Most Admired Men of 1971" list.

1972   Ralph Nader is again named to the Gallup Poll's "Most Admired Men" list.
Two biographies of Ralph Nader appear: *Nader: The People's Lawyer* by Robert Buckhorn, and *Ralph Nader's Crusade* by Richard Curtis.

1974   Ralph Nader edits CSRL's *Comprehensive Manual for Citizen Access to Federal Agencies*.

1975   Hays Gorey's biography of Nader appears: *Nader and the Power of Everyman*.

1976   Ralph Nader is placed on the ballot in Massachusetts as a presidential candidate. He demands that his name be removed, calls for a halt to export of hazardous products to other countries, and calls nuclear energy "a menace."

1977   Nader accuses Joan Claybrook, president of Public Citizen, Inc., of betraying consumers by supporting a Carter administration decision to allow automakers six years to install air bags in cars. Nader demands that she resign from this consumer watchdog group he founded.   She is later reinstated as president. Nader raises one million dollars in small contributions from the general public and speaks out more and more often about environmental pollution, nuclear energy, and fuel conservation.

1978   Nader fights in Congress to establish Consumer Protection Agency.

1979   Nader raises $1.5 million in small contributions and public appearances.

1981   Nader holds a $1,000-a-plate fund-raising gala for the tenth anniversary celebration of Public Citizen, Inc.
He proclaims the Reagan administration to be "my next Corvair."

1982   Dan M. Burt, in *Abuse of Trust*, alleges that Nader has never filed public disclosures required of all charitable organizations.
The network of PIRG supporters grows to one million people, many of them college students.

1983   Nader edits *A Citizen's Guide to Lobbying*.

1986   Nader's brother, Shafik, dies of cancer at home in Winsted, Connecticut. Nader gets Bell's palsy and must limit his lecture schedule.
Ralph and Claire Nader hire Ellen Thomas, a citizen activist, to save Winsted from overdevelopment.

1988   Nader works to stop apple farmers from using Alar spray on their crops. Public outcry results when FDA accuses it of causing cancer in children.

1989   Nader tells Congress that its members should not receive pay raises. While at first he persuades Congress, members later vote themselves raises. Nader begins fight to reverse that decision.

Index